Close to Home

One Orthodox mother's quest for
patience, peace, and perseverance

Molly Sabourin

CONCILIAR PRESS ∞ BEN LOMOND, CALIFORNIA

Published by   Conciliar Press Ministries
                P.O. Box 76
                Ben Lomond, CA 95005-0076

Printed in the United States of America

ISBN 10: 1-888212-61-6
ISBN 13: 978-1-888212-61-7

Cover designed by Carla Zell
Interior designed by Katherine Hyde

To my husband, Troy, and our children
for inspiring these stories,
and to Bobby and Paige
for drawing them out of me

Contents

Introduction

*I*n this book I will talk quite a bit about my husband and my children, so I'd like to introduce them to you now. But rather than rely on facts (e.g. Elijah's favorite song is…, etc.) that will surely change by the time this reaches your hands, I'd like to speak in terms of characteristics and quirks, which seem to better reflect the diversity and uniqueness of each individual within our household.

Troy is my spouse, my best friend, my partner. I married my opposite, and that has made for some challenging and exciting realizations about marriage, God, and myself. Troy sees no point in worrying, no justification for owning things we cannot  afford. He can walk into a crowded room where he knows absolutely no one and strike up a conversation without hyperventilating. He is dark-haired and tall with sharp, chiseled features. (Now imagine an individual who contradicts every single physical and behavioral trait I've just described and you'll have me in a nutshell.) Troy was an active adolescent who thrived on skateboarding, basketball and soccer. After college he pursued a career in social work, which fits his personality to a tee. He has a wry sense of humor and great taste in music. He loves the Church and his family. I am honestly more attracted to him now than I've ever been.

In 1999, I gave birth to *Elijah*, who, as you will soon discover, plays a major role in many of the chapters you're about to read. He is my firstborn, my first foray into every new stage of parenting. I find him delightful. If you stopped by our house today and  I introduced you to him, the chances are pretty good that Elijah would hug you. After that, he would talk your ear off, without stopping to take a breath or to ask if you'd come by to do anything else besides listen to him and his head full of science fiction facts. He would try his very best to make you laugh. Elijah has freckles, his father's slightly bowed legs, and my round eyes. He is a strong writer, much better than I was at his age, and is completely uninterested in playing sports. I am enjoying more and more our ever-deepening conversations as he matures and wonders with increasing urgency how exactly this Faith of ours works: belief and doubt, mystery and reason. He watches me closely for verification, which is simultaneously terrifying and incredibly inspiring.

In 2001, we welcomed *Priscilla*, who arrived, to our great surprise, a month early. For the first two years of her life, Priscilla observed. As an infant, she sat quiet and wide-eyed in her carseat, taking in liturgies, her brother,  dinner guests, and grocery stores. She chose not to crawl or scoot around, opting rather to sit upright in place while little friends her age crept on all fours in front of her. At thirteen months, she finally stood and started walking. I wouldn't have believed, had someone told me then, that Priscilla would be fiery and independent, a leader. She's as stubborn—no, determined—as an ant carrying twenty times its body weight. She will ride that roller coaster, master those skates, shovel that sidewalk, swim across that pool, win at that board game—just you wait and see! She will grab life by the horns without pausing every three feet to recalculate the pros and cons, the risks and benefits of diving into whatever opportunity lies before her. Priscilla is affectionate, creative, and empathetic to the pain of others. I marvel daily at her grit and imagination.

Benjamin arrived in 2002, a scant fifteen months after his older sister, Priscilla. "Irish twins!" people would say to me whenever I dared to go out in public with my three tiny children, aged four and under. He used to introduce himself as "the nicest boy in the world." He is snug-  gly and generous, which to me makes up for the mayhem and destruction that tend to follow in his wake. "BENJAMIN LEONARD SABOURIN!!" is how I usually call his name— how most people do if they spend more than fifteen minutes with him. Ben has fallen out a second-story window, cracked his head on our radiator, caught his clothing on fire while lighting a candle. But he is no worse for the wear and no less prone to skip, hop, leap, instead of walk, because of it. Ben is sensitive—easily hurt, but very forgiving. He is the only one of our children with my lighter coloring. He has vowed to always live in the same house as his parents, but I have a feeling the right young woman will be able to woo him out of that promise without too much effort. After all, his dream is to become a dad . . . and a fireman . . . and maybe a Jedi knight.

And last, but so not least (except in size), is *Mary Catherine*, born in 2005. Originally we were going to name her Elaine, until Elijah threw such a dramatic fit we finally said, "Fine. What do you think we should name her?" To which he replied, "Mary." Because, "If you name  her after God's mother, He will have to bless her!" And who in their right mind could argue with that? Mary looks just like Troy, if Troy were a Kewpie doll. She is drawn to all things girly and to sugar. She is completely unpredictable, quick-tempered, irresistible, and hilarious. She's an endless source of sparkly entertainment—a firecracker continuously exploding with volume and colorful brilliance.

The six of us make up *the Sabourins*—a family every bit as flawed and wrapped in grace as your own. What follows is the never-ending saga of our journey toward salvation. And while the stories are distinctly mine, I pray the underlying fears, frustration, bliss and hope are universal. It is an honor, my friends, to share these memories and discoveries with you.

Close to Home

Chapter One

Marriage

y dress was off-white and perfect. Worn only once before, twenty-eight years earlier by my mother, it reflected with its empire waist and flowing train a timeless elegance both simple and stunning. I fantasized about that dress and the sensation of its layered netting scratching my stockinged legs, the swishing sounds of taffeta serenading my every graceful step. I imagined myself as a princess lifted from the pages of a storybook; I imagined myself as a bride.

Just two months shy of my twenty-third birthday, I walked arm in arm with my weepy father down the aisle of the church my bridegroom, Troy, had grown up in. I was thinking that he looked handsome and my bridesmaids beautiful in their coordinating mint green shawls. I was aware of my high-heeled shoes pinching toes more accustomed to flip-flops, and of an impossible-to-reach itch beneath my carefully coiffed up-do, but that was the extent of my pondering. To be honest, I hadn't thought much beyond this magical day at all. My wedding was the culmination, the happy ending, the grand finale of my inexperienced life. My daydreams as a little girl had usually stopped here: in this dress and at this moment.

They (the already-married women) always tell a bride that her wedding day will be a blur, and the bride-to-be smiles politely, secretly confident that her wedding will be different, that she will remember every detail of that glorious occasion in slow, deliberate motion. Never again, in all likelihood, will she plan any other event with the same degree of passion, drama, and intensity. I was no different, and thus was quite surprised when my wedding day was over as soon as it had begun—my memories but a swirl of camera clicks and kisses choreographed to the tune of clinking glasses.

I had longed, more than for heaven itself, for a taste of the mysterious covenant known as marriage. What could be less lonely, less disappointing, and more fulfilling than sharing your life with a partner? If I could just hold on until the vows entwined us, linking us inseparably one to the other, then all my worries and insecurities would be buffered by the sharing of our love. Troy would complete me in a happily-ever-after sort of way.

I was groomed to believe this for as long as I can remember. Through fairy tales, love songs, romantic comedies, and a twenty-year dialogue with every other starry-eyed girl I knew, I became convinced that Prince Charming was out there, somewhere, pining for me as well.

Troy fit the princely profile of handsome, brave, and strong. Throughout our first fumbling conversations, freezing outside of a library after hours, I was giddy with the possibility that this could be "the one." My prince had a face, an identity, and a first and last name. I clung to the hope that the waiting was finally over, and that real life, better life, was just around the corner.

We met at Bible college, in a Genesis class to be precise. Troy did not fit the evangelical stereotype with his thrift-store sweaters, tattooed arm, and freshly earned scabs from skateboarding throughout Chicago every spare minute he could find. He was quiet, his thoughts fully occupied even then with doubts my mind could not yet comprehend. His uniqueness and unpredictability were refreshing to a girl burned out by the authoritative types, all too ready to engage her in theological discourse over sodas in the student lounge. Troy talked of God, incessantly, but with question marks instead of periods. There was desperation, beneath his seemingly placid exterior, for something more.

We struck up a friendship, exploring city streets, our commonly held convictions, and alternatives to the Protestant-style worship we had not previously stepped outside of for any length of time. When given the address of an Orthodox church ("An Orthodox what?" being my first reaction) by an acquaintance whose father was a priest, we hopped aboard a bus and journeyed to a world that was light-years away, yet located only a couple of miles from my dorm room.

To say I was shocked is an understatement. Everything throughout that period of time, while I was peering into the canyon of full-blown adulthood, felt urgent and intensified. Therefore, my senses nearly exploded from overstimulation when they encountered the richly vibrant sights, smells, and sounds of Orthodoxy.

While I cringed and sweated my way through our first Divine Liturgy, Troy inhaled the foreign-smelling incense like a narcotic. We departed after the service, both our heads spinning. I felt nauseous, but Troy felt eager for a little more exposure to this truly different interpretation of the Church.

I adored him for that, for his openness to new ideas, not realizing that what attracts us most to an individual is also, within the context of marriage, what usually becomes the most challenging characteristic to make peace with. When we were "friends," I enjoyed learning more about the incredible history of the Orthodox Church, but as our relationship evolved and our commitment to one another strengthened, these same conversations felt threatening.

After a year of dating, while simultaneously studying the Orthodox faith, it became evident that Troy and Orthodoxy would be a package deal. All I had learned about its symbolism, apostolic line, preservation of ancient Traditions, and theology-drenched hymnography impressed me, but I needed to be absolutely certain that these were my expanding appreciations and not mere echoes of Troy's enthusiasm.

After many catechism classes, dinners with new Orthodox friends, and dog-eared books on Eastern Christianity read late into the night between school assignments, I felt confident that I could make a decision to convert with authenticity. It was an enormous relief finally to embrace a future that involved both Troy and a faith that would later shape every thought, prayer, and desire I would ever have for the family he and I would one day start together.

Troy and I decided to marry in a church that would feel comfortable to our loved ones, with the intent of converting several months later. I couldn't bear the strain of seeing such a happy occasion as our wedding dampened by the confusion of family members. I wanted only tears of joy to glisten in the eyes of our guests as I floated past their pew in all my bridal glory. Troy conceded out of love for me, the first of a million compromises we would hurdle as husband and wife.

In hindsight, I feel a twinge of regret. After experiencing the Orthodox weddings of friends and acquaintances, I can't help but be impressed by that service's congruency with marriage itself. I was initially turned off by the ceremony's set-in-stone order and structure. I wanted the freedom to add my own personal touches to a ceremony focused on Troy and me.

After all, I had seen some amazingly creative weddings that included poetry, slide shows, surprise solos from husband to wife, and carefully crafted vows expressing the uniqueness of that couple's love for one another. And the length of an Orthodox wedding . . . oh, good gracious! I could just imagine my non-Orthodox guests in their three-inch heels shifting their weight and rolling their eyes. Why did it have to be so different? The crowns, the lit candles, the processions, and the haunting hymns felt too foreign to me at that time.

But now, after eleven years of marriage—and after passing through the honeymoon phase and wading through the nitty-gritty everyday details of being one with your spouse and yet altogether different from him simultaneously—I can see how all the symbolism, all the seriousness, and all the scriptural references woven throughout a wedding ceremony that is distinctly Orthodox set an appropriate tone for the intensity of life ahead. I can appreciate how the uniformity from one Orthodox wedding to the next coincides with the uniformity of God's intentions for all married couples—to spur one another on toward salvation. I can understand quite clearly why this sacrament must revolve less around the bride and groom, and more and more and more around Christ.

I remember sitting at a restaurant with Troy just hours after our cake-and-finger-food reception earlier that afternoon. With all the hullabaloo of planning and celebrating behind us, we were at something of a loss as to what to do next. The conversation felt awkward and forced ("Nice wedding, huh?"). I was still in ideal mode, and worried a bit that the warm tingling passion I'd assumed would electrify us both from the moment we said "I do" had not kicked in as expected. I was confused as to why in these first hours as a wife I still felt insecure, as if at any moment I could say or do something stupid to make him love me less.

After a week in the Smoky Mountains, where we spent our honeymoon terrified by pitch-black skies, howling coyotes, and winding roads up to ear-popping altitudes, I looked forward to starting life, real life, as a team; I looked forward to reveling in our intimacy. Without realizing it, I shifted all my hopes, my self-esteem, and my longings for contentment onto one imperfect man. A dangerous combination of wanting to please and yet wanting to be pleased resulted in some initial passive-aggressiveness on my part.

"Do you care if I go out with my friends tonight?" Troy asked me once early in our marriage. I did care. I didn't want to be alone on a Saturday night. I didn't want Troy to prefer their company to mine.

"That's fine," I lied, "I mean if that's what you want to do." Knowing of course that he would read my mind and refuse to leave without me.

"Great! I'll call them," he said, pecking me on the cheek while reaching for the phone. I, in turn, pouted my way through the next two hours with grunts and one-word answers.

"What's wrong?" he asked.

"Oh . . . nothing," I sighed, and then stood up dramatically and started to wash the dishes.

"All right, then. See ya later!" Without batting an eye, he took off for his guys-only evening.

As the door closed behind him, I sobbed in disappointment. I felt completely overwhelmed by loneliness. I had, essentially, put all my eggs in one basket, a basket Troy had dropped because it was altogether much too large for any human being to carry. When he came home to find me crying, he wrapped his arms around my shoulders.

"What happened?" he asked, alarmed.

"How could you leave, when you knew I had no plans?

Why didn't you want to spend a quiet night with me, your wife?" I blubbered.

Instead of apologizing, Troy pulled back his arms and looked sternly at me. "I asked you if it was okay for me to go and you said yes. I asked if anything was wrong and you said no. It is not fair for you to say one thing and mean another. I need us to be honest with each other!"

Ouch. The truth held up in front of you like a big old mirror in unflattering light is never pleasant to look at, but there it was, plain as day: I was wrong to think that Troy should bend over backwards to interpret my emotions. I was naïve to hope that marriage would fill a gap in my soul created to overflow with adoration for God.

Two people trying to live by breathing in one another will find out soon enough that the oxygen is limited. Their love will inevitably fall victim to suffocation. Every married couple eventually gets to the point where the rose-colored glasses through which each had viewed the other are shattered. It is common in this day and age just to assume, then, that the match was a poor one, that someone else is out there who is capable of saying and doing all the right things to keep you satisfied—all the things your old partner couldn't.

It is at this crucial stage that the difference between marriage as a sacrament of the Church and marriage as an expression of affection between two individuals becomes most significant. It was at this crossroads within my own marriage that the death of romanticized misconceptions made way for the resurrection of a miraculous and unconditional love rooted in divinity.

"There is no relationship between human beings," said St. John Chrysostom in his homily on marriage, "so close as that of husband and wife, if they are united as they ought to be." He goes on to say:

Paul has precisely described for husband and wife what is fit-ting behavior for each: she should reverence him as the head and he should love her as his body. But how is this behavior achieved? That it must be is clear; now I will tell you how. It will be achieved if we are detached from money, if we strive above everything for virtue, if we keep the fear of God before our eyes. What Paul says to servants in the next chapter applies to us as well . . . knowing that whatever good anyone does he will receive the same again from the Lord (Eph. 6:8). Love her not so much for her own sake but for Christ's sake. That is why he says, be subject . . . as to the Lord. Do every-thing for the Lord's sake, in a spirit of obedience to Him.

Between the years of 1997 and 1999, I became a wife, an Orthodox Christian, and a mother; all three of these roles were challenging. My marriage went through several meta-morphoses at breakneck speed in order to keep up with the changes. By the end of that twenty-four–month period, I was much too tired to be flawless. But in the midst of admitting I had no idea what I was doing; in the process of shedding old skin to make room for the new me growing and evolv-ing with each trial; with the realization that my husband could not save me from the frustration of reaching my own limits, I found the desperation necessary to throw myself at the feet of Christ. I began to internalize the teachings of St. John Chrysostom and discovered that when my identity was wrapped up in my role as a Christian, when love for God was the source from which my thoughts and actions originated, I was more apt to support Troy with no strings attached. When I trusted in my own shallow resources, however, my love became possessive, manipulative, and self-serving.

With the onset of parenthood, Troy and I had to become reacquainted all over again, now as "mom" and "dad." We had different backgrounds and different ideas about discipline and job sharing. I felt it was unfair that his life did not change as severely as my own, and he felt limited as to what he could give to a baby obsessed with its mother. Our words became poorly aimed arrows, usually missing their mark. I was too emotional to be taken seriously, I figured bitterly, and he was too removed from my existence as a lonely new mother to offer the right advice or comfort. Orthodox Christianity was the one common denominator in our lives. Communing together, fasting together, and standing as a couple before our icons in prayer fueled our desire to keep trying, to keep giving, to keep sacrificing ourselves for the sake of salvation—to obey Christ by serving one another.

Troy and I each desired respect for the positive elements we were bringing to this marriage and to this family. I had to force myself to inquire about his day and really listen, asking questions that confirmed my care for and pride in his ability to persevere within a stressful job environment. I had to pause and mull over my grievances, determining while calm whether or not they were worth a confrontation. If so, I had to proceed with carefully constructed explanations (rather than loud, impulsively fired assaults on his character— assaults that we would both surely regret) and remain open to the criticism I would receive in the process.

I had to pray every morning for wisdom and correct thinking, for divine guidance as to when to assert myself and when to hold my tongue. I knew that the natural outcome of a healthy marriage was healthy children who would not settle for anything less than being treated with loving respect by their own potential partners down the road. I knew I wanted to show my kids that Troy and I were a united team, incapable of being divided.

Troy is a very attentive father; I have fallen in love all over again with this new, older man beside me, transformed by the hardships and pleasures of providing for his family. I am especially sensitive now to the slow, steady drifting apart that can occur due to inadequate communication; I pounce on the widening gap between us and stitch it back together with prayer, apologies, and forthright conversation. We invest ourselves in this marriage, making frequent deposits of affirmation, unprompted kindness, and extemporaneous hugs and kisses. Troy and I make it quite clear there are times when he and I are not to be interrupted. We teach our kids by example that the relationship between moms and dads must be cultivated with time and effort, that giving us space to bond and catch up after a long day apart is beneficial for everyone.

I am proud of Troy, and he is proud of me. Out of that mutual pride flow courage, stamina, and a continuous yearning for improvement. The sacredness of our marital covenant only deepens as the years pass and as the obstacles of raising four spirited children test our faith and commitment to one another.

Marriage is never static. This miraculous relationship must be nourished or it will wither and die of starvation. It must be watered with sweat and tears in order to bloom and bring beauty to its household. The healing effect of a sincerely offered compliment from Troy never ceases to amaze me, nor does my own power to return the gift of encouragement with reciprocated words of heartfelt appreciation. May we never, when our children are grown and gone, look upon one another as strangers who have lost their one connection, their only adhesive whose absence makes evident two separate hearts beating out of sync and shivering in the frigidity of love grown cold. May the sacrament of marriage purify our souls and always remind us that God is good.

Chapter Two

Conversion

I can feel it coming, the dramatic pause and raised eyebrow at my response to the conversational inquiry about where my family and I attend church. Especially if this question is a follow-up to the obligatory, "Where did you go to college?" or "Where did you and your husband meet?" I understand the confusion and try my best to buffer the blow that this Bible college graduate has indeed converted to Orthodox Christianity.

It has been over ten years since Troy and I made that life-changing decision, taking part in front of our family and friends in the service of chrismation on a cold afternoon in January. This ancient sacrament officially confirmed our desire to join the Eastern Orthodox Church through the receiving of chrism and the Holy Eucharist. As we stood there, foreheads and feet glistening with fragrant oil, I felt certain that the door I had been knocking on for the past two years had opened at last, to this place, at this moment, by the grace of God.

In 1995, "Orthodoxy" was not the controversial buzzword within evangelical circles that it is today. As far as I knew, no other American Protestant had ever considered living out his or her faith within the confines of this often-stereotyped cultural backwater. If anyone had told me that within a decade I would be praying with icons, taking part in confession, and witnessing the baptism of all four of my babies, I would have shaken my head and walked away, dismissing my fortune-teller as mentally unstable. I knew that I struggled with being a square peg in a round hole, but I figured I would keep looking within Protestant circles for a pew I could nail my heart to.

I grew up with a firm belief in the death and resurrection of Jesus Christ. My family attended church every Sunday morning, and I was a regular attendee of Sunday school, church camp, Vacation Bible School, and high school youth group. All of these experiences validated my conviction that I was loved and known by God.

As I entered my teenage years, this faith remained integral to my actions, thoughts, and decisions. Although I wrestled with the common moral dilemmas associated with adolescent independence, I never doubted God's existence or His role as benevolent Creator and Savior of the world. I had no interest in church history or theology. The idea that martyrs had been tortured, councils established, and nations split over the structure and essential foundation of the Church and its teachings was simply not applicable to a seventeen-year-old girl in the throes of soured love, part-time jobs, and college applications. Jesus was my confidant, my frame of reference, and my friend.

After graduating from high school, I enrolled at Moody Bible Institute, a well-known and respected Bible college in downtown Chicago. I didn't have a good handle on what I wanted to be, or do, or study, and this small, close-to-home, conservative institution seemed like a safe place for me to break out on my own.

Freshman year, every student takes basically the same core classes. The course names on my schedule sounded harmless enough, but I was ill prepared for the mind-blowing experience I would soon enter into as I was trained and tested in the tenets of Systematic Theology, Christian Life and Ethics, Personal Evangelism, and Church at Work in the World. There was more to Christianity than just "me and Jesus," apparently, and my heart and intellect collided in the endeavor to sift through the many opposing doctrines being tossed in my lap for scrutiny. I had been introduced to Calvinism, premillennialism, "Lordship salvation," and "easy believism."

Within every classroom, dorm room, or student lounge, heated debates were testing newfound convictions on women in the church, speaking in tongues, the end times, faith vs. works, and free will vs. predestination. I was envious of my classmates who were able to pick a path, strap on some blinders, and walk confidently without hemming and hawing at each fork in the road. I missed the old days, before everything was so complicated; but like a child who has seen her father eat the Christmas cookies left for Santa, I couldn't trust any longer in the simplicity of my childhood beliefs.

After two years at Moody, I became a notorious church-hopper. Most of my attendance decisions were based on convenience, and with all the time I spent in chapel, missions conference, and the annual Founder's Week Bible conferences, I didn't feel it necessary to plug into any one community.

By this point I had lost the shiny idealism I entered with, and I accepted or dismissed theological beliefs with the streamlined precision of an experienced seminarian. The biblical interpretations were endless, and it was up to me, through prayer and study, to decide which pieces I would mold together to form my own complete manifestation of truth. When it became evident that no single church catered to all my Christian beliefs and preferences, I chalked it up to ignorance and started sleeping in on Sunday mornings.

By that time I had started dating Troy. We shared similar frustrations and a conviction that Christianity must contain elements we had not experienced thus far. Sometimes we would make the effort to peek outside our familiar circumference and take in a Lutheran, Episcopalian, or even a Catholic service. The pomp with which they handled the Gospel, recited their litanies, and lined up for Communion both intrigued and unnerved me. The God I knew so intimately was being handled with kid gloves, and I questioned the need for such formality. How could they sincerely worship without varying the music or the sermon series, or without spontaneity in their prayers? Surely, these scripted responses were dry remnants of denominations out of touch and out of sync with modern culture. Hadn't the Reformation freed us from a works-based belief system and breathed life into the cold, dead liturgical groaning of the Middle Ages?

The winter semester of my junior year, I was given the assignment to attend a church service and evaluate its musical style. Troy had in his notebook the address of an Orthodox church in the city that he had been given by a student at the University of Illinois at Chicago. He had been on that campus conducting religious surveys for class, and started a conversation with a young man whose father was an Orthodox priest. Troy had recently read a book by Bishop Kallistos Ware, entitled *The Orthodox Way*, for his History of Doctrine course, and was curious now to see this unfamiliar Liturgy in person.

That Sunday we took the bus to Holy Trinity Cathedral. I will never forget the awe and fear that nearly took my breath away as we opened the heavy, wooden doors and peered for the first time into the extravagantly foreign depths of Orthodoxy.

The Orthodox Church caters to the senses of its members. Visually, it is a feast for the eyes. As the Old Testament temple was splendidly lavished in precious metals, silk, and jewels, so does the Orthodox temple create an environment of heavenly opulence designed to rescue our thoughts from earthly cares and focus our attention on the Kingdom of God.

Icons, representing the "great cloud of witnesses" referred to in Hebrews 12:1, fill the sanctuary with their faith unashamed and fervent desire for this generation of Christians to "run with perseverance the race set before us." Priests serve in vestments that vary in color, depending on the seasons of the church calendar. The Gospel book and communion chalice are ornately adorned in gold. A fog of incense softens the brightness and adds to the mystery, reminding parishioners with each inhalation of the final days in Revelation when Christ, enthroned in all His glory, will be worshiped by every created thing.

Upon first visiting, one's ears are assaulted by the strange drone of chanting woven throughout the services. All prayers and scripture readings are sung in monotone, allowing the words to speak for themselves without the distraction of personal inflection or dialect. The clergy speak and dress in such a way as to maintain anonymity. They do not face the people but rather turn toward the altar, standing together with the congregation in reverent adoration of the Holy Trinity.

Every church I had attended growing up felt safe and warm in its familiarity. The sanctuaries looked much like my own living room; the kind pastors were approachable in their sport coats and dress pants. The choruses were upbeat and melodic.

The contrast on that Sunday was shocking. I did not get the sense from Holy Trinity Cathedral that I was welcome to come in and be ministered to. It was I who was expected to do the participating. The two hours we spent standing in the balcony seemed to drag on forever. My feet were aching, I couldn't understand the order of the service, the smell of incense made my head spin, and the *a cappella* hymns and chanting reminded me of a cultic ritual. The clergy with their synchronized movements in and out of altar doors, swinging censers, and kissing of hands, books, crosses, and icons resembled the mechanized villagers I had once seen dancing in rotation on a giant Swiss cuckoo clock.

When Troy and I finally made it out to the safety of the street, I looked at him to confirm my suspicion that whatever was going on in that place was purely heretical. On an otherwise solemn face, however, I found in his eyes a spark that burned like a single twig glowing beneath a pile of dry embers.

I can't remember if either of us said much in summary of our experiment. Troy, having read one book on the subject, was able to provide at least enough clarity for me to eke out my school paper. I did not plan on ever returning and hurried back to campus reveling in the predictability of my comfort zone.

While Troy quietly checked out more information, I wrestled with questions sprouting up in my thoughts at random intervals. Why had I never heard about the Orthodox Church before? Where did it fit in historically? How could God be there, and with me at the same time?

I stepped up my church attendance, determined to find peace in a sedately gorgeous brownstone chapel within walking distance. I appreciated the literary references, intellectual ponderings, and century-old hymns sung by the black-robed choir at my new place of Presbyterian worship. Its stoic and subdued demeanor seemed less emotional and more respectful of God and His divinity. If I liked the sermon that week and the song choice of the choir, I would leave fulfilled. If, however, the sermon failed to connect with me personally or the hymns felt too dry to quench my spiritual thirst, I would try to take comfort in the hordes of other churches lining the streets of this great big city, waiting to meet my needs. Often this attempt at reasoning, however, would backfire by confirming that I was too picky, too demanding, and dangerously close to giving up altogether on ever feeling satisfied.

Troy and I continued to date, becoming more serious about each other over time. The topic of Orthodoxy sprang up with greater frequency in our conversations, and Troy's factual tidbits began gnawing their way into my psyche, distorting my assumptions of what defined the Church. We read with heightened interest about the Great Schism of 1054, when the original Church established by the apostles split, East from West, over the final straw of the *filioque* (the addition made by the West to the Nicene Creed). While the Western church went on to split thousands of additional times, starting with the Reformation, the Eastern Church remained intact, using the same Liturgy, sacraments, and structure of leadership it had for the previous fifteen hundred years. The Orthodox Church was, indeed, out of touch with modern culture. Walking through the doors of Holy Trinity, I had entered a time warp and encountered a living artifact of antiquity.

Partly out of curiosity and partly out of love for Troy, I agreed to a few occasional visits over the next couple of months. Armed now with some basic knowledge and historical context, I wavered between heartfelt appreciation for this symbolically saturated sneak peek into early Christianity, and feelings of cold, clammy terror that even this silent observation was a blasphemous act of betrayal. I mumbled along to the Nicene Creed, the "Lord have mercy's," and the Lord's

Prayer, but my lips snapped shut at the mention of Mary, and my arms stiffened in protest against the notion that I should join others in crossing myself. "What do You want from me?" I prayed, over and over, without any real hope of an answer.

After Liturgy, Orthodox church members generally gather for a time of fellowship aptly named "coffee hour." Anyone receiving the Eucharist on Sunday must fast from food and drink starting from midnight the evening before. To replenish themselves, they visit over plates of doughnuts, fruit, or bagels, washed down with steaming cups of coffee. Troy and I had thus far successfully avoided getting lured into one of these, but after about four non-consecutive Sundays of hiding in the balcony, a gray-bearded doctor named Peter flagged us down. He was so kind and animated we didn't have the heart to refuse him, and so we tagged along to meet in person the church body my egotistical young brain had already summed up as distant and superstitious. Dr. Peter set us down at a table by a couple not much older than ourselves, with a six-month-old baby. Joshua was welcoming, friendly, and quick-witted. Janine was very sweet and sincerely interested in how we had ended up at the fellowship hour of an Orthodox church.

Joshua's father had been a priest, so he was very knowledgeable about church rubrics, Tradition, fasts, and feasts. He had also briefly attended Wheaton College, a nondenominational conservative Christian college, before returning to Orthodoxy as a young adult. To our relief, he was comfortingly aware of what would most alarm us and what aspects of the faith would require a thorough explanation. Before we left, Troy and I scheduled a time to get together at their small apartment just two blocks away.

Inside my head, throughout this time, was a scary place to be. I felt literally sick to my stomach as I imagined the faces of friends, family, and professors, narrowing their eyes and turning down the corners of their mouths, demanding an explanation for this foolishness—an explanation I was in no position to give. I had nothing to stand on but a thin strand of hope, and even that was fraying under the weight of a potentially earth-shattering decision looming in the future.

Lunch that next Sunday was laced with inner tension. I was there to put Orthodoxy on trial. I wanted Joshua and Janine to defend their faith and their mode of worship. I was taken aback by their quiet confidence and easygoing manner throughout a conversation I now look back on as something of an attack. Why did they use icons? Why did they venerate Mary? Why did they believe in asking the saints for intercessory prayer?

Never once did they turn the tables and rub in my face the disjointed factions within modern evangelicalism and the unchecked freedom it had claimed to spawn updated views of the Gospel, changing the medium and the message as it saw fit. Joshua calmly provided clear, historical, and logical reasons for each practice I questioned.

I started to understand that lining up Protestantism alongside Orthodoxy was like trying to compare apples and oranges. Orthodoxy was planted and grew in persecuted nations, comfortable with the allowance of mystery. If you asked an Orthodox Christian if he or she was "saved," for example, you would not get a neat, cut-and-dried, yes or no answer. Christianity, for the Orthodox, is seen as an organic whole, no one discipline or principle being defined outside the context of another. In the booklet, "Am I Saved?" (Light and Life, 1984), Fr. Theodore Bobosh explains salvation this way:

The question, "Are you saved?", appears to some to be shallow. It seems to imply all that is needed is to say yes or no. Yet we also know that Christ taught us to take up our cross daily and to follow Him. Christ told us to strive to enter into Salvation (Luke 13:24). Christ has indeed accomplished His work for our Salvation, but ours is just beginning.

This answer, borderless and free-flowing, did not come with a money-back guarantee that my name would be written with permanent ink in the Book of Life, but it certainly did seem to make good sense. If salvation were just a one-shot deal, why go through the grueling effort to counteract every innate tendency toward self-preservation in order to become empty vessels for Christ? Why did St. Paul describe salvation as a race to be run with perseverance?

If I accepted the Orthodox position of salvation as a process, it would not be within my jurisdiction to make judgments on the sincerity of my fellow athletes. I would be chiefly responsible, rather, for evaluating how effectively I was using my unique gifts and circumstances to glorify God, working out my *own* salvation with fear and trembling (Phil. 2:12). Of course I would still believe in God's goodness and limitless mercy; but I would remember my place as a servant and never assume ownership of such an amazing gift.

Being so accustomed to arrogantly picking apart everyone else's faith, I had never realized the toll this habit was taking on my own spiritual life. I had lost, or perhaps had never even discovered, the awesome and mysteriously indefinable Gospel message. Perhaps Christianity needn't be pinned down and organized in outline form. Maybe Christ's teachings didn't fit neatly in my predictable square box. That day my view of God exploded, shattering the barriers I had placed around Him and opening doors I never knew existed, hidden behind the heavy tapestries of Western culture.

Troy and I got engaged in December of 1996. I knew,

without a doubt, I wanted to spend the rest of my life with him. But I was nonetheless miserable in that the road ahead was foggy and treacherous. My hunger for this bigger God compelled me to take another step forward, but I wanted to carry along my evangelical safety net, even as it tangled around my feet and hindered my movement. I desperately desired the best of both worlds. Troy, in the meantime, had silently cut ties with his past and prepared to venture forward, come what might. This tension loomed between us, threatening a permanent separation.

I was in no man's land. Through reading, attending regular Orthodox services, and conversations with new Orthodox friends, I had learned enough to seriously entertain the possibility that the Orthodox Church contained within it the Truth intact as passed down from the apostles. There was still so much, however, that I had not come to terms with, and I was terrified to turn my back on my evangelical past, which had been so influential in shaping my Christ-centered worldview. I couldn't go back, and I didn't think I had it in me to move onward. The more confident Troy became in his decision to join the Orthodox Church, the more I resented his courage, my fear, and even God Himself for presenting these choices without identifying the correct one with a big green check mark.

Holy Trinity was offering catechism classes for those who were interested in learning more about the Orthodox faith. These were taught by a good-natured, frighteningly intelligent, and refreshingly rational long-time social worker named Tom. Together we went through *The Orthodox Church* by Bishop Kallistos Ware. Tom was funny and unbelievably knowledgeable. I still cannot fathom how one head could contain the ocean of facts he knew, not just about Orthodoxy, but about history, literature, and culture as well.

Tom's approachability helped me relax, and I felt confident asking tough questions, knowing he was incapable of being offended. When asked why all the emphasis on Mary, he explained how her role as Theotokos, or "God-bearer," protected the dogma of Christ's being fully human and fully divine, which had been called into question during the early centuries of Christianity. Mary had always been revered as the first Christian and as the supreme example of submission to God's will. When the Roman Catholic Church introduced the doctrine of the Immaculate Conception (formalized as dogma in the nineteenth century), Protestants overreacted by reducing Mary's place in the plan of salvation to that of a seasonal backdrop for Christ's glory.

Tom also explained how the Orthodox eagerly petition saints to intercede for them, not because the saints are seen in any way to be equal with Christ in power and authority, but because Orthodox Christians view the boundary between this life and the afterlife as a curtain rather than a brick wall. Since these holy men and women had fought the good fight and were most definitely in the presence of the living God, Orthodox Christians could ask for their prayers, just as we would ask a friend or family member here on earth to pray to God on our behalf. *The Great Divorce* by C. S. Lewis illustrated beautifully for me the concept of death being an extension of the life we are now living.

These controversial issues, when actually studied and poked at, proved to have value and substance. By no means was I on board with everything I heard, but I was at least finished with assuming that any Orthodox practice I found difficult to understand automatically equaled heresy and spiritual treason. Each week, I was warming up to the idea of giving up the fight and resting in the strong arms of this Church. Troy and I went forward with wedding plans, looking forward to the day when we would be joined together in name and in faith. When it became obvious that a conversion was imminent, our families bravely offered us up to God. Their faith, despite a legitimate fear of the unknown, revealed a deep conviction of Christ's sovereignty.

There was still so much I didn't know. It would take a lifetime to familiarize myself with the symbolism, church calendar, musical tones, and so forth. At first I was concerned about my lack of passion for Mary, the saints, and weekly fasting. What I had gratefully accepted, however, was a sincere belief that the Orthodox Church held within herself unchanging Truth miraculously passed through thousands of hands, both good and evil, in periods of peace and of intense persecution, without compromising the teachings of the church fathers or bowing to modernity. I was confident that my compliance would be rewarded with a genuine reverence for these facets of Orthodoxy as I grew in knowledge and practice.

Orthodoxy is not easy. Many have jumped with fervor into her fullness, only to drown ultimately from a lack of stamina. Orthodoxy should be savored slowly, taking bigger bites as your appetite naturally increases, not swallowed whole in one big zealous gulp. Having a spiritual father was invaluable in helping me to understand the spirit over the letter of the law. My priest lovingly guided me through my transition from a checklist-driven faith to a fluid, sacramentally fueled devotion to becoming a little more like Christ every second and with every circumstance put before me. Whereas before I had been in the habit of urging God to come down into my life, I now sought to enter into His.

In humble amazement, over the years since our conversion Troy and I have attended the chrismation services of one friend or family member after another. To worship alongside my brother, my parents, my college roommates and their husbands and children is nothing short of miraculous. What once seemed impossible is now the most real thing I know.

My eight-year-old son, running out to meet the bus, stops dead in his tracks and yells, "Mom, what about my blessing?"

I approach him, smiling, and make the sign of the cross over his heart. "May the Lord God bless you," I say, "in the name of the Father, and the Son, and the Holy Spirit." I pray as he departs that this small physical act of invoking the grace of the Holy Trinity, translated in his mind as motherly love, will stay with him and his siblings, not just today, but for eternity.

Chapter Three

Pregnancy

I told myself I would not buy the test just yet, even as I walked out of my way to pass a drugstore while coming home from work. Eyes lowered and blushing, I handed eight dollars to the teenage boy behind the counter, who rang up my purchase without an ounce of interest in the blue-and-white box tossed casually into a plastic shopping bag.

"Do you want your receipt?" he mumbled.

"No, thank you," I said, leaving the proof of my impulsive purchase in his hands.

I opened the door to an empty apartment and quickly buried the test in my dresser drawer beneath piles of socks and underwear. There was dinner to start and laundry piles to wade through, but even as I vigorously chopped and sorted, my thoughts became riddled with curiosity; the tension of not knowing was more than I could bear. Before self-discipline had the chance to intervene, I darted for the bathroom, test in hand.

Up until this point, I had convinced myself that any result would be just fine by me. I was young, only twenty-four years old, and Troy and I had been married for less than a year. I figured we could certainly use a little more life experience before diving into the awesome responsibility of parenthood. But sometime within those three eternal minutes of waiting for the test to register, my desire to have a baby became magnified. Hormones I never knew existed were raging for a chance to reproduce.

The color was faint, a soft gray compared to its bright blue neighbor. But sure enough, it was a pair of lines that stared back at me. Blood rushed to my tingling head, and I could hear the nervous beating of my heart. For the past four weeks, while I had been working, eating, sleeping, and running errands, a child had been forming in my belly. Life would be different, starting now.

There was no possible way I could concentrate on anything, so I sat in anticipation, listening for Troy's footsteps down the hall. I would try to be nonchalant, to pay attention as he summarized the many details of his day before unloading my massive bombshell and changing his life forever. But when he stood there before me, all those carefully chosen words leapt out of my mouth before I could catch them. Holding out the positive test, I watched the news sink in and a timid smile spread across his face. We embraced, of course, but had I known the entire truth about children, and parents, and faith, I would have clung to his chest a little longer. I would have lost my right to be giddy with pure, unadulterated elation.

I have always been a sucker for pregnant women. As a little girl, I stuffed pillows into T-shirts and studied myself in the mirror. I couldn't wait for a real baby bulge to beautifully round out my waistline. Even now, I can go months without hearing the tick-tock of my biological clock, only to come across a waddling stranger in maternity jeans and think, "Aw, maybe I should give it another go."

Every day I looked for changes in my body. Some mornings I would question if it were even true, given my still flat stomach, and I would dig out the pregnancy test in order to confirm that I wasn't crazy. It was not until a doctor validated that positive result and congratulated me on becoming a mother that I began to tell coworkers and acquaintances the exciting news. It wasn't until I was confident my baby existed that I began obsessing over the possibility of losing him.

The glass of wine I'd had a week ago, the mauve-colored polish chipping off my nails, the ibuprofen I'd taken for a headache were poisoning my unborn son, I was absolutely certain of it! I needed information, and fast! Wearing a path in the carpet at our local Barnes & Noble to the section on pregnancy and birth, I read every theory, opinion, and strategy on the best way to carry, and eventually deliver, a baby.

My vocabulary evolved into a language unrecognizable to my husband. "Doula," "Bradley method," "folic acid," and "epidural" were just some of the mysterious mothering code words thrown into everyday conversation to the annoyance, I am sure, of all my non-mothering friends and family. In fact, the only people whose eyes didn't glaze over, but rather brightened with recognition, were other mommies-to-be navigating the same murky waters while trying not to drown in the flood of advice from experts profiting off our nervousness.

The sudden need for community became all-encompassing, and I searched every bookstore, grocery store checkout line, and coffee shop for swollen ankles or a carefully wrapped baby sling. "How far along are you? How old is she? Is he sleeping through the night?" My seemingly tame and unobtrusive inquiries were often mere cover-ups for the real questions I was dying to ask: "How many pounds have you gained? Does your baby sleep in bed with you? Are you afraid of becoming undesirable to your husband?"

Pregnancy introduced me to a whole new level of vulnerability. I had previously let down my guard, exposing a soft and tender underside, for the sake of love, friendship, and spiritual enrichment. But on all of those occasions, it was only my emotional well-being at risk, and I decided ultimately where, when, and for whom I would shed my hardened exterior. But while housing within my own fragile body a life and spirit separate from my own, my "personal" decisions began to feel heavy with the weight of added responsibility.

My protective shell cracked into a million pieces from the expansive pressure of an average-sized heart ballooning with concern for a baby. No matter how extensively I prepared, or how many hours I researched, I could not guarantee a favorable outcome. I could not be certain that my child would be healthy, or that he would even survive through nine months of development. I couldn't be sure of my own health or of my ability to endure labor. Without recognizing it for the universal maternal trait that it was, I bristled at my newfound anxiety, and I chastised myself for the sleepless nights filled with horrific possibilities.

And there were horror stories, all right, plenty to go around. "My sister-in-law suffered through twenty-two hours of labor only to end up with an emergency C-section," a stranger in an elevator once told me.

"Well, thanks for that," I thought, picturing myself passed out cold on an operating table.

The most excruciating encounter hit closer to home, however, when an old friend came by to visit. She had recently lost her daughter due to the umbilical cord strangling the baby's tiny neck in the last month of pregnancy. I honestly wanted to pray only for her, as she showed me the photos of her baby shower and empty crib, but so quickly came the pleadings from my own soul to God to be spared that same tragic fate. I was terrified of being punished for my selfishness.

What I wanted were statistics, some cold, hard numbers to support the easily forgotten reality that most pregnancies, most births, and most babies turn out just fine. I looked forward to my upcoming prenatal check-up, where I was sure my doctor would smile and shake his head. "Oh, Molly," he'd say, "you are a young, healthy woman. That little one inside you is perfectly safe." So I spilled out my fears, sounding extra pathetic, to my physician, who happens to be a very devout Orthodox Christian (yes, I know, lucky me!).

"Well," he said, "babies die and mothers die. It happens all the time. Being pregnant requires a lot of faith."

Truth be told, I hated that answer! Praying was, let's be honest, a last resort. First, you ate right, took your vitamins, refrained from caffeine and alcohol, had every ultrasound and amniocentesis test insurance would allow, and studied enough information on baby stuff to earn a master's degree in . . . well, Baby Stuff. Then you started in with the "Lord have mercy's."

I grew up believing that Christianity was a sanctified version of secular life. I strove for the same goals as everyone else: happiness, success, and financial stability. There were a lot of "bless me" prayers. "Please bless this (day, relationship, decision, etc.)." I would do the footwork and actual planning, and then God would come forward and seal the deal. I was not yet used to this newfangled idea of handing everything over, of having no personal control over the outcome of any given circumstance, of accepting the unknown without trying to manipulate it into something more palatable. How anyone could go through the sheer, miraculous insanity of becoming a cocreator without asking herself some serious questions about life and death was beyond me. A tiny human being was kicking at my rib cage and opening my eyes to a bigger God and a broader understanding of His mercy.

In February of 1999, just weeks before Elijah's birth, I attended my first Forgiveness Vespers. The fasts and feasts were still a mystery to me, as I had never before paid notice to any kind of church calendar. I remember that the novelty of being pregnant had worn thin; my lower back ached with just the thought of standing through yet another service. But Troy and I attended, at the urging of our bishop, kicking off a Lent that would change everything. Somewhat timidly, I kissed the cheeks of fellow parishioners, prostrated by lowering my neck, and asked for the forgiveness of everyone in attendance. It was quite possibly one of the most beautiful events I had ever witnessed. I rejoiced in the traditions, such as this one, we would pass down to our son, now head dropped and ready for his great entrance into the world.

But even then, I quivered at the thought of teaching a theology I was still only learning myself. Pregnancy, like Orthodoxy, was so much bigger than the breadth of my current understanding. Whatever previous confidence I had stored up in terms of skills and capabilities was leveled once I took that first giant step off the beaten path, once I held my breath and ventured forward down a pitch-black road miraculously illumined just seconds before each twist and turn laid out before me. What appeared, initially, to be a finish line—becoming Orthodox and pregnant—would turn out to be a starting block on which I knelt in anticipation of the deafening explosion that would declare the race had begun.

Looking back on those months, on those weeks while I prepared to be a mother, a part of me wishes I could whisper into my own younger ears some crucial information about the future. With that foreknowledge in hand, I am sure I would have wasted less time weeping over spilled milk and stepping gingerly over nonexistent land mines. But usually it's the process, rather than the end result, that proves to define our values and our character. Knowing the answers would not have stretched and limbered up my faith as did offering up my heart and my hands toward Christ, out of adoration, out of obedience, out of fear of the unknown.

It seems to me so very compassionate that God became Man as He did. In His giving Mary the choice to say yes or no to the bearing of Deity in her womb, the relationship between the Creator and His creation became one of reciprocal love. Mary's answer to Gabriel's burning announcement that she would carry a Son to be called Jesus, without ever knowing a man, is the ultimate example of submission: "Behold the maidservant of the Lord! Let it be to me according to your word."

Never having revered Mary, I was initially quite self-conscious when face-to-face with her icon as a newly illumined Orthodox Christian. The prayers of intercession I brought before her felt thick and unwieldy in my throat. It seemed silly and shameful for me to adjust her rank from Christmas card scenery to the most Holy God-Bearer, Theotokos, in one month flat. I begged the Lord to help me understand her, to fire up warmth for her in my soul.

Thanks be to God, the ice began to melt when I felt, for the very first time, stirrings of life in my abdomen. The lines of communication began flowing as I laid out before her thoughts, concerns, and hopes surely she, as a mom, would understand. Talk about no guarantees—Mary's future after accepting her fate, her honor, her joy, and her grief as the mother of Jesus, God's Son, was as open and overwhelming as a rowboat floating in the ocean with no land in sight. Her belief in a God as invisible to her as the wind rocking waves with authority should bring courage and comfort to all of us who feel small and vulnerable in our own little boats, weathering each frightening storm as it comes.

As the sobering days of Lent came to their quiet conclusion, Elijah's own jabbing movements settled in preparation for delivery. I was longing for new life in the form of birth and Resurrection, my soul and body equally weary from carrying such heavy loads. There are many women for whom pregnancy is like a shot of adrenaline. With superhuman strength they tear down guest room wallpaper, sprint through the aisles of Babies-R-Us, and break open boxes of gifts containing diaper genies, exersaucers, and strollers.

I, unfortunately, am not one of them. For me, that last trimester is neither pretty nor productive. Between my pulsating veins, puffy eyes, and generally crabby demeanor, I find it extraordinary that Troy, my sweet husband, never once jumped ship while I sank into the excruciatingly endless abyss of waiting for the first pangs of labor.

There are very few occasions necessitating the total pausing of everything—work, travel, plans, and the millions of nagging tasks buzzing about my brain like pesky flies. Holy Week and the week before (or after) a baby's due date are two of them. Both events are so very effective at pushing me past my limits, at forcing me to acknowledge my weaknesses. With the trusty safety net of everyday distractions removed, the tightrope on which I try to balance suddenly feels too high and narrow to ever get across on my own. My efforts to fast, pray, and delight in the treasured and holy moments of stopping to acknowledge God's omnipotence take me only so far before I lose steam and then stall like an overheated car by the side of the road, watching everyone else, it appears, drive on successfully toward their own destinations.

"Just come already!" I want to scream while mixing up yet

another batch of hummus or pulling out the same stretched-out maternity shirt I wear every other day. "Before my lack of energy, self-discipline, and enthusiasm ruin such a glorious event!"

But on the plus side, there is never an ounce of confusion. I have yet to participate in either a birth or a midnight Pascha service wearing any false notions of pride. The tears of relief and true happiness rolling down my cheeks are that much sweeter knowing Christ Himself picked up my slack. Because only when the imposing brick wall that signifies both the end of myself and the beginning of my humility stands solid and impassible but an inch from my sullen face, do I remember to call out for His mercy. And only then, when against all human odds, I am standing on the other side where light and forgiveness poke holes through foggy skies, where the Kingdom of God sparkles without bias on the paths of those who devote their hearts, minds, and spirits to finding it, can I accept that new life is bestowed, rather than manhandled or manipulated into existence.

All the walks and castor oil in the world could not coax Elijah from the warmth and security of his mother's womb. When the nineteenth of February came and went, I honestly tried to make peace with the fact that I was doomed to be pregnant forever. I dreamt one night that while riding in the car, my baby, after seven long years, finally decided to make his appearance. Gripping the armrest and clenching my teeth, I pushed out, to my great surprise, an adolescent child who immediately upon his arrival requested something to eat. I was trying to swaddle him, to contain those impossibly long arms and legs so they'd fit on my lap. I loved this boy but was still so very disappointed at having missed out on his infancy, at not remembering his cries, his smell, his first attempts at communicating.

I think of this now as Elijah practices baseball in the back-yard, as he rides his bike and yells to his friends that he'll be right over to play. On those sweet occasions when he spontaneously runs up and hugs me, when he wraps me in those lanky limbs all tan and smooth save for the scabs and downy hair below his knee, I try to remember. I bring out photographs of ages and stages that seemed sure to last forever, but all of the stress and chaos become muffled by the echoes of mispronounced words and high-pitched giggles.

It never gets old to me, the amazing truth that God stitched this completely independent person currently begging me for thirty minutes of computer time, with perfection from out of nothing. David, in Psalm 139, beautifully expresses his own sense of wonder at the intimacy of our relationship with God:

> For You formed my inward parts;
> You covered me in my mother's womb.
> I will praise You, for I am fearfully and wonderfully made;
> Marvelous are Your works,
> And that my soul knows very well.
> My frame was not hidden from You,
> When I was made in secret,
> And skillfully wrought in the lowest parts of the earth.
> Your eyes saw my substance, being yet unformed.
> And in Your book they all were written,
> The days fashioned for me,
> When as yet there were none of them. (Psalm 139:13–16)

Is it all that shocking, then, that we are commanded to love our neighbors? Once we understand God's role in our creation, does it not make so much sense that He desires us to look on every single person with at least a fraction of the care and concern that went into their very formation? Does it not seem like a grievous insult to despise or give up on ourselves when our origins were so strategically engineered? Is there anything more encouraging, when the aftermath of our mistakes or the mistakes of our children seems altogether insurmountable, unfixable, and unforgivable, than remembering how invaluable is our worth when seen in the light of God's craftsmanship, within the context of His great and eternal plan?

Chapter Four

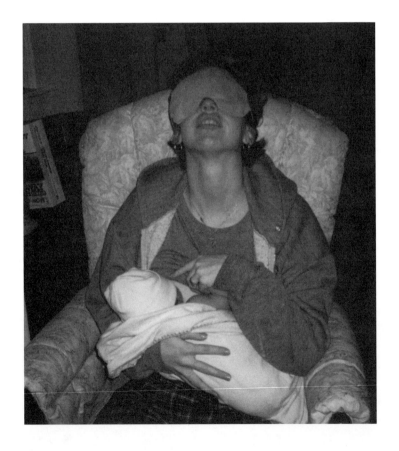

Birth

hen babies arrive one right after the other, like coins from a twinkling slot machine spilling generously into outstretched hands, memories tend to blend and blur in all the excitement of corralling such an explosive treasure. My kids love to play the game where we sit around the kitchen table and guess who did what adorable thing as a wide-eyed infant or precocious toddler. While the stories are always accessible, bubbling in my heart like a geyser of nostalgia, it is a struggle to remember exactly which of my children ate Play-doh, sucked their toes, or was leery of stepping onto the "alligator" to get from one shopping level to the next.

But what remains remarkably clear to me, untouched by the dizzying tornado of recollections ripping through the years with too much speed, is the nitty-gritty details of an afternoon in February when I first experienced the thrill and agony of giving birth. That day, so vivid with significance, was unforgettable.

Due to my aversion toward needles and hospital gowns, it was decided early on that I would have our baby at home, and by home I mean a three-room basement apartment in downtown Chicago with floors so slanted we put hockey pucks under the feet of our bed to keep it level. Most women, my friends assure me, see birth as something intimate and private, an event to be witnessed by only a husband, a doctor, and perhaps one's own mother if she can keep herself together without hovering over the medical staff trying to do their job. I did not, for some reason, pick up on that preference and thus ended up with a large gathering of friends and relatives snacking, whispering, and waiting while I began the arduous work of coaxing an eight-and-a-half–pound baby out of my uterus and into the world.

At six-thirty A.M. on the twenty-third of February in 1999, I awoke to the telltale tightening and cramping that signaled labor had begun. Within the hour I was counting through painful contractions while my best friend and sister-in-law kept track of the time. Two weeks earlier I had been sent home from my doctor's appointment with a large, sealed box with the words, "To be opened by medical personnel only!" printed boldly on its front and sides. I stared at it for days, wondering what kind of pulleys, elixirs, or prayer ropes had been packed inside for this very occasion. I was relieved when the nurses calmly walked in, ripped open the mystical "home birth box," and brought out sterile bandages, alcohol swabs, and a standard-issue blue-and-pink striped hat, too tiny to comprehend. Three hours in, and our place was packed. The sounds of normalcy kept me from panicking as the intensity and nausea that gripped my back and forced my heaving head into a bucket became unbearable.

Finally, after eight hours of inching, stretching, and burning through my insides, our baby was ready to meet me. It's funny the things you think you remember when in a state of altered consciousness. I was sure, for example, that I had been screaming like a banshee, but was told later on that what sounded to me like a frenzied siren of alarm fell limp from my mouth in a whimper.

The pressure seemed likely to kill me, so I pushed with all my might to find relief in either death or the exodus of this child. And then, whoosh! There he was, shiny and red as an apple, rooting on my chest for nourishment only I, his mother, could provide. I cried for all I'd been through and in thankfulness for all I'd received—a ten-fingered, ten-toed miracle named Elijah.

The euphoria that followed, as estrogen and oxytocin rushed through my bloodstream and heightened my senses, came as close, I am guessing, to a drug-induced high as I would ever experience. I was wider-than-wide awake, stronger than a tigress, and more jubilant than a six-year-old on Christmas morning. Elijah was passed around the room like a trophy while I, the triumphant victor, looked on with pride—laughing, eating, and attempting to walk on legs of jelly.

"Take it easy," warned the nurse, having before seen such deceptive confidence reach its high-pitched crescendo before crashing.

"You take it easy," I thought. "I am indestructible."

"*I think* he is losing weight, Molly."

"Why are you saying that?" I was terrified and offended by my mother's observation.

"Go ahead and call the doctor," she said.

Elijah was only three days old. Everything about him now scared me: his tight rosy skin, his bleating cry, his anxious mouth desperate for milk that for some reason was building up with force in my breast but could not make it through his lips and into his starving belly. This is not what I had imagined at all, even a week ago, when I was big and ungainly, exhausted from carrying beneath my ribs and on top of my bladder a full-grown infant.

I actually said these clichéd words to my mother and sister-in-law, while rocking my screaming newborn: "Why didn't anyone tell me it would be like this?"

There are an awful lot of mothering misconceptions lining the aisles of Babies-R-Us and stylishly adorning the catalogue pages of Baby Gap and Pottery Barn Kids. It is legitimately exciting to daydream about nursery colors and coordinating bedding, but there is a reason the miniature gingham sheets and the matching bumper in the picture are so pristine: newborns don't actually sleep on them, not for months. She will sleep on you, like a cat curled up on your neck (only not as soundly), but the cherry-wood monstrosity, complete with prison bars, that keeps her from smelling, tasting, and feeling you will most certainly be shunned. It also turns out that the teeny-tiny sport coat will never be as big a hit with your son as the hand-me-down footed jammies, worn and soft with use.

I had never seen all that goes on behind closed doors—the doors that divide mothers from the bigger world outside. In my trendy Chicago neighborhood, there were few stay-at-home moms surviving their days one feeding at a time. All I knew were happy moms, pretty moms, and wealthy moms with decorated houses. Moms I had seen on television, or heard interviewed, or read about in the pregnancy magazines layered like a fan on my coffee table. "This is the greatest role of my life," they'd always say. "How rewarding! How fulfilling! How wonderful!" I couldn't wait to get in on the love.

In the examining room of my doctor's office is a poster that perfectly depicts my own expectations during all those weeks of monthly check-ups and invasive prodding. A woman with flowing hair, wearing a floral sundress, is nursing her baby in a garden. She is glowing with adoration for the pink bundle in her arms, which is staring up at her and brushing her cheek with a delicate fist. That woman would be me, I thought, patient, matronly, and naturally beautiful. I imagined my son and myself walking the city streets. I would be wearing my skinny-girl jeans and he would be sleeping contentedly in the BabyBjörn. We'd take in an art museum or visit my non-mothering friends, who would marvel at how adorable we both were.

You can imagine now, understanding my state of mind, how duped I felt when motherhood initially turned out to involve a lot more flabbiness, wetness, scariness, and loneliness than happiness, fulfillment, and fun. This baby boy was no accessory on my hip. He was more like another organ, a second heart perhaps or a third lung, feeding off my blood and oxygen. As we were so intimately connected, his needs became my needs. When he couldn't nurse, I would howl in pain. When he couldn't sleep, I lay wasted with exhaustion beside him. When he needed to be held, skin to skin, I needed it too. My hormones would cry out in desperation, "Get that baby! Hold him! Inhale him! We need the fix, and fast!"

In my photo box, a big blue Rubbermaid tub, is a letter I keep to remind me of my maternal metamorphosis. In the wee hours of an icy morning in 1999, serenaded by the low and steady hum of the breast pump, I penned an emotional outcry to my husband.

Dear Troy,

I am writing this because I love you and you deserve to know all that I am feeling. I fear that every day I distance myself from you a little more because I don't know how to share with you the intensity of my emotions. The other reason I write this is that I fear trying to explain this verbally will only result in you thinking I am nonsensical.

Troy, I have never felt so scared and alone in all my life. It scares me to be with the baby sometimes because I fear that I will just give up. The feedings, the pumpings, constantly changing his clothes, recording every move he makes in a log, weighing him, dreading the phone calls from the lactation consultant, never leaving the house, never wearing clean clothes, the prospect of never sleeping through an entire night—it is simply too much to deal with by myself. When Elijah loses any amount of weight I feel like such a failure. I often find myself being resentful, thinking it is solely up to me to handle every responsibility having to do with our baby. Here is where our communication seems to fail us. I know that you feel stress about your job but since I am so caught up in myself, I don't really listen. I have no idea what you think about or what you have been doing all day. It is like we live in two separate worlds.

I need you so badly but I don't know how to ask for help without sounding like a nag. I love you so much. Every night I watch you sleeping and thank God that He brought you to me. Our marriage is so precious and I want to make this transition into parenthood together as a unified team.

I hope this hasn't confused you. If so, let's talk about it.

With all my love,
Molly

Several things strike me when I read this, so many years later. I have to laugh at the part about watching Troy sleep because it sounds sweet enough until you take it literally. I was observing him from the couch, nearly crazy with jealousy, as his chest rose and fell in slumber. What I see, in my own handwriting, is the painful shedding of skin, the ripping of immaturity from my character. I am reminded of why the phrase "no pain, no gain" applies to so much more than athletics. I want to go back and wrap my arms around that girl, scared to death of the responsibility before her. I want to tell her that she is doing nothing wrong, that the frustration is part of the process.

It took awhile to understand that love and learning were two different experiences. I could simultaneously adore my child and grieve the loss of freedom. I could struggle with the requirements but still want the position. Motherhood wasn't segmented, squared off with borders, like my nine-to-five job or electronic calendar. It was fluid and transitional, free from the limits of time, logic, and reason.

There are many moments as a mom when I feel spent and wasted. I ache for my children and for my own limitations. I am sorry for not having more to give. But when you look at it realistically, there are bound to be days like that. Are we not human and imperfect? As mothers, we aren't scored by the number of dishes washed, onesies folded, or hours spent swaying back and forth in a rocking chair. I can tell you, with certainty, no one is watching—a fact that brings comfort as well as despair.

Our "success," rather, is measured internally. A good day is one in which guilt is not the victor. A successful day is any day when we fall, get up, and then try again; such resilience is absolutely essential for our physical, emotional, and spiritual well-being. After reading it on an Orthodox website (orthodoxchristian.blogspot.com), I have clung to the following dialogue, which for me parallels a mother's obligations, pares down the peripherals, and captures the true essence of living one's life for Christ:

A young monk complained to the great ascetic Abba Sisoes: "Abba, what should I do? I fell."

The elder answered: "Get up!"

The monk said: "I got up, and I fell again!"

The elder replied: "Get up again!"

But the young monk asked: "For how long should I get up when I fall?"

"Until your death," answered Abba Sisoes (source unknown).

Our defeat is not assured by the number of times we inevitably screw up, but by failing to hope in our Lord's mercy.

For a week I fed Elijah with a medicine dropper. Carefully, I would hold him in my lap, his fuzzy head elevated slightly on my knees. I pumped my breast milk into jars and offered sustenance as best I could, one little drip at a time. The days were long and tedious. But the delight I felt with each ounce gained came bubbling up from the chasms in my heart. Eventually he learned to latch on. I could do away with the nipple shields, breast pump, and dropper. As with my letter to Troy, however, I couldn't part with the feeding logs. They were too symbolic of our progression, too powerful a reminder that perseverance precedes courage and contentment.

"Why didn't anyone tell me it would be like this?" I still mutter those words almost daily. But of the few things I have learned, through tears, experience, and the wisdom of other women—real women pacing themselves through this soul-refining adventure—there are a couple I feel obligated to share.

The first is that motherhood will look and feel absolutely nothing like the life you led previously. You cannot compartmentalize children. I often read in bios that so-and-so is, oh, let's say, an award-winning journalist, an author, a gourmet cook, and a mother of two. This is so very misleading. You are always a mother first. Your child or children will infuse every single element of what you do, what you think about, what you dream about, what you eat, and what you plan for. Particularly for those of us who stay at home without nannies or housekeepers or sometimes even family support, the demands of feeding, dressing, cleaning, playing, comforting, teaching, and transporting will at first overwhelm you. It will sometimes feel as if you live in a bubble; you can see and hear the outside world, but you are not a participating member.

The second is, you can do it! You will juggle life's responsibilities with one hand, one eye, and one ear in order to hold your baby, see what he or she is into, and listen for cries of help. There are many days you will feel totally and utterly incapable, and you will look around the room for backup, for someone else to step in and let you take the break you so desperately need. When you realize there is no such person and your kids are still hungry, or sick, or tired, you will dig deep and pull up a tiny reserve of strength you didn't know you had. This, my dear friends, is growth. No other job in the world is more effective at chiseling you into a stronger and more competent person.

Each of my four births presented for me a situation requiring more wisdom, peace, patience, and energy than I currently had at my disposal. When our third child, Benjamin, was born, a mere fifteen months after the birth of his sister Priscilla, I was terrified. Troy had just started graduate school, adding new stressors to his already demanding full-time job as a social worker. We were living in a cramped two-bedroom condo, and I had no car to escape my pavement-surrounded island of isolation. I was, essentially, right where Christ wanted me to be: in a constant state of prayerful dependence on Him. Only from there could I properly see

my infant in light of the gift that he truly was—not as a possession, not as a hobby, and not as a thief of my identity, but
as an opportunity to wrench from my soul that which keeps
me mortally distracted, focused on my needs, my wants, and
my desires.

Father John Breck, a professor of biblical interpretation
and ethics at St. Sergius Theological Institute in Paris, gave
a lecture at St. Tikhon's Monastery in June of 2002, entitled
"The Sacredness of Newborn Life." In it he expanded on the
significant relationship between Christ and a newborn baby.

*Who, in fact, is this newborn child we are called to welcome,
protect, nurture and love? He or she is the image of Christ,
the Son of God, who—"without change"—became the son of
Mary, for the salvation of the world and the deification of all
those who receive Him with thanksgiving and devotion. "To
all who received Him," the evangelist John tells us, "to all those
who believed in His name, He gave power to become children
of God" (1:12). To become a child of God is to return to our
original state of innocence, purity, beauty, but also of vulnerability, which characterized the first human person, fashioned
in the image of his creator. This is the "Adamic state," proper
to every newborn child. Yet it is a state soon lost in a world of
sin, where the innocent, inside or outside the womb, are mas-
sacred like the little children of Bethlehem.*

*The newborn child bears within himself the divine image,
the image of Christ, and with that image comes the possibility
for deification. But this tiny infant also bears within himself
the seeds of corruption. The continuous and arduous struggle
between the two—between deification and corruption—will
lead him inevitably along the pathway of suffering and death.
The newborn child is an image of the Christ-child; but he is
also an image of Christ crucified.*

Every day I have the choice to either forget or remember. I can forget that my faith is the greater reality and resent the constant struggles—despising the heaven-sent opportunities for strengthening my fortitude instead of learning from them. But if I choose the latter—remembering how relevant to my salvation is every wiped nose, every sleepless night, every apology for losing my temper, and all the other acts of submission that chip away at my stubbornness and unite me to Jesus through my unconditional love for the newborn, the toddler, the eight-year-old who finds security in my arms and reflects the very image of Christ—I will find purpose and satisfaction in this role as a parent.

I don't kid myself by expecting perfection or by thinking that someday I will master the art of being a mother. There is no final destination, only a lifelong journey. But I take very seriously the speed with which the years pass by, understanding that my involvement in the interior lives of my family members takes priority over every other commitment in my life. I owe it to my children and to my husband to be gentle on myself. I set the tone for our household. When I give in to self-criticism, everyone's mood is dampened; but if I can find peace (oh, what a gift!), our home becomes light and joyful.

Chapter Five

Baptism

I know that I wore a white cotton gown and that it was big, way too big for my kid-sized body. I was after all only nine years old, an appropriate age within my Protestant faith community for getting baptized. I know there were others, adults mostly, gathered around our pastor on that Sunday evening ready to declare their devotion to Christianity, ready to tell the world, or at least the twenty or so parishioners in attendance, that they were followers of Jesus Christ. I knew, as I was holding my nose and being lowered into the lukewarm water, that I was joining a legacy of faith. I knew I loved God. And I knew that when all of this was over, my family and I were going out for ice cream.

Up until somewhat recently, all this "knowing" seemed very important. And although the details were fraying at the edges, it was significant that the overall experience had remained intact, that I could remember it with ownership and certainty. I had chosen (at my parents' urging) to identify in this symbolic way with the death and resurrection of Jesus. And since that's how I understood it, as a response to salvation rather than as a miracle in and of itself, it seemed only logical that a reply of "Yes, I will choose to believe" would come from a mind mature enough to understand such a decision. Into my adult years, I carried with me a definite respect and appreciation for the baptismal service in which I had participated as a child. But if you backed me into a corner, I would be forced to stop short of referring to that event as "necessary" for salvation, since I believed the only truly non-negotiable requirement was an acceptance of Jesus as my Savior.

Within this particular mindset, the baptizing of an infant would be troubling to say the least, since the most important element of salvation—the individual's decision—is completely sidestepped. It would appear as if the baby were exempt from any personal accountability: "Poof, there you are (splash, splash, splash) . . . a Christian!"

The Reformers fought vigorously to disentangle Christianity from the "for-profit" hocus pocus of the Middle Ages, where tickets out of purgatory could be bought for the right price through indulgences. Naturally we, as their spiritual descendants, remained skeptical of anything that could possibly be misconstrued as an abuse of clerical power, such as a priest declaring a baby "justified" without his ever having repented of his sins or expressed a desire to follow Christ's teachings.

Yet even with these concerns firmly in place, I was secretly fascinated by the idea of babies, clad in angelic white, being cradled in the vested arms of a somber priest. It seemed appropriate to me that the phenomenon of a newborn infant, already in possession of a soul, would be acknowledged with great fanfare and seriousness. Too bad the entire premise of it was so off the mark theologically. In other words, I just really liked the looks of it in a forbidden, secret kind of way, like being attracted to a dark and mysterious stranger you would never actually date or dream of bringing home to meet your parents.

Imagine my joy, then, when I finally became Orthodox, when I immersed myself in this apostolic tradition and began viewing my Faith—including salvation, death, confession, and baptism—within the context of the mystery and antiquity that is Eastern Christianity. Imagine my relief at being able to adhere to the original calling of the Apostle Peter, "Repent and let each of you be baptized in the name of Jesus Christ for the forgiveness of your sins" (Acts 2:38a), without having to interpret it in light of Roman Catholicism, without having to distance myself from the viewpoints of errant ancestors. I was free for the first time to embrace wholeheartedly this sacrament I had previously admired guiltily from afar.

The more I understood about its original purpose and significance, the more in awe I became of Christ's intimate connection to both the physical and spiritual lives of His children. When the time was approaching for me to become a mother, I studied the Church's view on baptism with a new desperation, a more personal motivation to have clarity on what exactly, within my child, would be altered by this act of obedience, by my offering of this most holy and precious blessing back to God.

Of the many "Aha!" moments after my conversion, one of the most momentous came from reading through a helpful booklet published by Conciliar Press, aptly titled, "Infant Baptism." The author notes Scripture passages that command entire households (not just mothers and fathers or children over the age of seven) to be baptized. He also includes excerpts from the teachings of church fathers and teachers such as Irenaeus, Hippolytus, and Origen, clearly condoning the practice of babies "being washed with water and the Spirit" (Origen, Commentary on the letter to the Romans

5:19). But I was most blown away by the author's own explanation of salvation and its relationship to "understanding":

> *From Genesis to Revelation, the witness of the Scriptures is clear that when all is said and done, salvation comes to us through the mercy of God. We are not saved by understanding, by decisions, by works, by prayer, or even by "enough" faith—as important as these things are. What adult, for example, truly understands the mystery of baptism and union with Christ? Who among us has perfect trust in the Lord? Faith is always maturing. Father Alexander Schmemann writes, "The Orthodox Church, radically different from some 'rationalistic' sects, has never posited 'understanding' as the condition for Baptism. She would rather say that true 'understanding' is made possible by Baptism, is its result and fruit, rather than its condition"* (Of Water and the Spirit, p. 18).

Of course! Of course! Thank goodness, of course! It wasn't I, at the tender age of nine (overly concerned with getting water up my nose), who had initiated my own salvation through baptism. It wasn't I, at five years old (overly concerned with ways to avoid bedtime), who had the wherewithal to open my heart to God through nightly prayers, which "invited" Him down from heaven and into my life.

God was GOD! For so long, too long, I had viewed Him as a partner. I adored Him, I was loyal to Him, but the line between our roles as caregiver and dependent had been smudged by a misconception that I, in fact, had chosen Him, had responded of my own accord. How much more humbling and reassuring to realize that the Holy Spirit in all His glory, despite our irrefutable selfishness, out of pure and unconditional love, lights within our hell-bent souls a spark of salvation through baptism, which is then ours to either fan or snuff out. Father Anthony Coniaris, in his book, *Introducing the Orthodox Church*, writes:

> *Baptizing infants before they know what is going on is an expression of God's great love for us. It shows that God loves us and accepts us before we can ever know or love Him. It shows we are wanted and loved by God from the very moment of our birth. To say that a person must reach the age of reason and believe in Christ before he may be baptized is to make God's grace in some way dependent on man's intelligence. But God's grace is not dependent on any act of ours, intellectual or otherwise; it is a pure gift of love. (Light & Life, 1982, p. 129)*

Elijah was exactly forty days old when I packed a diaper bag with a tiny gold cross, a towel, and a white cotton gown, much smaller than mine had been. The previous week had been a busy one with the assigning of side dishes, salads, and desserts for a reception to follow the main event, which was to take place at Holy Trinity Cathedral. A million thoughts ran through my mind: "Will the water in the baptismal font be warm enough? Will I know where to stand and what to do? Will there be plenty of food? Will our friends and extended family members feel too uncomfortable with the service to enjoy any of it? Will I enjoy any of it with all of these cares and concerns distracting me?"

At that moment, in the midst of such once-unimaginable details, I was reminded of how far I had traveled over the last two years. Life is funny that way, taking us inch by inch into places often foreign and frightening, moving deeper and deeper into the thick of it as we learn to adjust, as our eyes begin to focus, as our ears start to recognize the language.

Until one afternoon you gaze up with attentiveness at the entirely new surroundings in which you find yourself and gasp with wonder, "Well, who would have thought I had it in me?"

This was my sentiment on that early spring morning, preparing my son (and myself) for that most special occasion. It was almost like an out-of-body experience, like observing from afar the packing, the menu-planning, my life as an Orthodox Christian. Not only was I a mother, a fact weird enough in itself, I was a mother who firmly believed that her highest priority was to raise her child in the Church—to initiate that salvific relationship through baptism.

Our priest, Fr. Joseph, was an imposing figure—a monastic with a stern face and a tenor voice—clear, melodic, and strong. Holy Trinity Cathedral was itself quite imposing to anyone unfamiliar with Orthodoxy, with the glow of beeswax candles within heavy golden stands and with the life-size painted icons on the walls. As our invited guests started trickling in, most were visibly shaken by the strangeness. They smiled, they hugged, they unequivocally supported us, but I knew (and who could blame them!) that warning bells were reverberating against their centuries-old distaste for that which smelled of ritualistic magic. Within Protestantism, within America, such pomp and formality are generally regarded as neither necessary nor appropriate.

I felt for them; I wanted more than anything to assuage their fears. I longed for everyone I loved to feel the joy and the gratitude that I did. At that point (and sometimes at this point still) I was not able to express verbally why Troy and I had chosen this path, not only for ourselves but now for our children as well. In my head, in my heart, and on my soul, the reasons were etched with clarity, but in my mouth they got all jumbled and confused. All I could do was to live it, the sacramental life that had saved me from the triviality of self-preoccupation, and trust that God would warm the hearts of others through the ways in which I had changed: the painful shedding of my often-bristled exterior and of the arrogant assumption that I was a "good enough" disciple of Jesus Christ.

Fr. Joseph held Elijah in the crook of his arm, casually, naturally, as if babies were an element commonly included within monasticism. I was thinking that my son looked unusually miniature in the folds of Father's black cassock while he explained to us the order of the service. It would start in the narthex with my churching (a set of prayers welcoming me back into the life of the Church after forty days of staying home to heal and bond with Elijah), and then the baptism would actually begin.

"Blessed is the Kingdom of the Father, and of the Son, and of the Holy Spirit, both now and ever, and to the ages of ages. Amen." I felt chills up my spine as Fr. Joseph's heavenly voice filled the sanctuary with purpose and authority. The litanies that followed included prayers for illumination and for deliverance from tribulation, evil, and distress. These were not warm, fuzzy, watered-down wishes for a cute and cuddly baby, but rather a passionate acknowledgement of sin and death and their combined potential to sabotage salvation—Elijah's salvation being taken with the utmost seriousness.

"That he may preserve the garment of baptism and the earnest of the Spirit undefiled and blameless in the terrible Day of Christ our God, let us pray to the Lord," chanted Fr. Joseph, giving words to my fervent longings. The water was then blessed: "Manifest Yourself, O Lord, in this water, and grant that he that is to be baptized may be transformed therein to the putting away of the old man, which is corrupt according to the deceitful lusts, and to the putting on of the new, which is renewed according to the Image of Him that created him, that, being planted in the likeness of Your death through baptism, he may become a sharer of Your Resurrection."

Within the next forty-five minutes, Elijah would be anointed with chrism (signifying the sealing of the Holy Spirit—Acts 8:14–17; Exodus 30:22–25), plunged three breathtaking times into the font, inundated with scripture readings from the Books of Matthew, Romans, and Psalms, and tonsured by having a small lock of hair (of which he had plenty!) snipped and then burned as the first offering of himself to God.

In every baptism I have been fortunate enough either to participate in or to witness, the tears in my eyes predictably start escaping when the infant is carried three times around the font while the choir sings liltingly, "As many as have been baptized into Christ have put on Christ, Alleluia." At this point, mid-service, I am overwhelmed by the beauty, the intensity, and the meticulousness put forth by the Church for the benefit of one tiny person. I rejoice in the significance of each of us. Finally, when Fr. Joseph laid Elijah on the steps leading up to the altar, the service concluded and I stepped forward to embrace my newly illumined son.

I was officially now in uncharted territory, raising a child who would be Orthodox from birth. By submitting him to Christ in this manner, Troy and I had agreed that we would raise him in the Christian Faith. We had acknowledged our intent to produce generations of Orthodox Christians and agreed to do everything within our power to encourage Elijah, through our prayers, example, and participation in the sacraments, to respond to the love planted in him that day through the grace of our Lord Jesus Christ. And thus the adventure of a lifetime commenced, starring a quiverful of spirited children, my husband Troy, and myself.

There are those who find salvation in monasticism, still others who are called to be clergy; there are men and woman who lay aside selfish ambitions to serve the Church financially or through physical labor. And then there are parents, whose exciting, exhausting, rewarding, and humbling call to populate the world with godly and righteous offspring will test their own resolve to be purged from the sin that entangles. From that day forth, I would enter through the doors of our parish as part of a family. I would be responsible for explaining to my son elements of a liturgy I, too, was just learning. I would be frustrated with his short attention span. I would be humbled and moved by observing his partaking of the Eucharist. And I would ultimately mature out of necessity, through my failures and determination to try again.

The reception was lovely. Elijah slept soundly even while repeatedly being exchanged from one set of arms into another. We took so many photos—way more, I am ashamed to admit, than were snapped at Priscilla's, Benjamin's, and Mary's baptisms combined. My favorite, to this day, is a black-and-white shot (which you can see at the beginning of this chapter) of a towering Fr. Joseph raising a delicate, dark-haired Elijah high into the air after his first vigorous dunking. He is seated in the palm of Father's large hand, strings of water still connecting him to the font below. Visually it is stunning. Emotionally it is stirring. Spiritually it is inspiring, a reminder to stay focused on my most essential obligation as a mother.

Sometimes, when I wake up in the morning, I expect to find that raven-haired baby in his crib, because I swear that picture was taken just yesterday. But somehow, Elijah escaped what I once considered a perpetual state of infancy, and now he is out of control, growing like mad, a freak of nature with all that excessive development trying to morph him into a man. Elijah's evolution certainly puts things in perspective. His burgeoning independence is a reminder to play baby dolls for a few extra minutes with his two-year-old sister and to look his six-year-old brother smack in the eye when he's recounting his most outlandish dream sequence. It motivates me to linger on the couch, snuggling seven-year-old Priscilla, who is chomping at the bit to be as big as her older brother. Elijah, already encountering ideas about life and its ultimate purpose vastly different from the ones we carry with us as Orthodox Christians, rouses my efforts to incorporate our faith into every single element of their being.

Priscilla and Benjamin have their game faces on; their toes are right up against the starting line (a crack in our bumpy sidewalk). They are there to run, they are there to win, and are anxiously awaiting my signal. "Ready, set, go!" Full of adrenaline, the two of them pound the pavement, undistracted by the goings-on in our neighborhood. This is doable, you see, even though they are naturally inclined to lose their focus, because the race has a definite starting and endpoint. They have the drive to persevere because they can see quite clearly where they've begun and where they are ultimately heading—in this case, the stop sign on the corner.

It isn't meant to be a maze, our path to the kingdom of heaven, but one can sure get lost in the turning and twisting byways of overthinking. Do I have to be baptized? What exactly about that process saves us—the water? the prayers? the oil of holy chrism? How much is required, after the fact, to hold onto the gift of the Holy Spirit?

And we, in receiving Baptism, . . . conceal ourselves in [the water] as the Savior did in the earth: and by doing this thrice we represent for ourselves that grace of the Resurrection which was wrought in three days. And this we do, not receiving the sacrament in silence, but while there are spoken over us the Names of the Three Sacred Persons on Whom we believed, in Whom we also hope, from Whom comes to us both the fact of our present and the fact of our future existence. (St. Gregory of Nyssa [ad 383], Sermon for the Day of Lights)

Notice that the facts of our present and future existence are made known to us not by logic or careful analysis, but only through the Names of the three Sacred Persons on whom we believe and in whom we have placed our hope. "Thy will be done," is all we must say; it is the crux of what we should teach our children. When Christ, in no uncertain terms, linked baptism with salvation, our starting point was, quite mercifully, revealed to us. What more effective means is there for learning how best to run the race than by actually running it? I promise you, it is not by scrutinizing the course, studying the weather conditions, or by observing the swiftness or slowness of other runners that revelation will be acquired, but rather through obedience and humility.

In their baptisms, each of my kids has a moment he or she can point to with absolute certainty, an assurance that before they could possibly earn such a blessing, God loved them. "This is the day," I can say without hesitation, "that hell and death lost their power to defeat you; this is the day you were marked as justified and illumined. Not because of magic words, not because you deserve it, not because Mom and Dad are already Christians, but because Jesus is perfect, because God became Man, because Jesus offered Himself for your sins and rose from the dead. And now take that spark within you and protect it, stoke the heavenly fire in your soul, use the tools God gave us—prayer, fasting, confession, Holy

Communion—to grow in faith and finish what was started on the day of your baptism. And then love, love others as Christ loves each and every one of us—without bias, without limits, without restraint."

Chapter Six

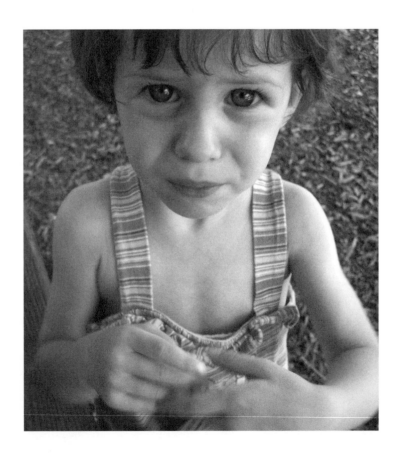

Disappointment

When I was pregnant with Elijah, I would watch the mothers in our parish come and go through the nave door like extras in a musical—off stage, on stage, changing their tunes with each new entrance. Each mother starts off cheery, putting down the diaper bag, setting up camp in her usual spot—close enough to see but a little to the side so that quick getaways will not be blocked by the fellow parishioners now clucking and cooing at the bundle of sweetness in her arms.

It only takes ten minutes, however, for the baby's whimpering to interrupt the solemn flow of liturgy. "Sh-h, sh-h," whispers mom, swaying like a reed in the wind (back and forth, back and forth, back and forth). But when the whimpering noises linger, despite the rocking, mom and baby head for the door for a diaper change, a nursing session, or simply for a distraction.

Act two begins five, maybe eight, minutes later. Mom is still smiling, but she rolls her eyes for the benefit of those she passes. "Babies," her facial gesture communicates, "what can you do?" (back and forth, back and forth, back and forth)

"In peace, let us pray to the Lord," chants the priest.

"Lord, have mercy," we respond. And mom sings also, into the little ear all soft and downy snuggled up close to her mouth. But her baby isn't that keen on settling down or giving in to the sleepiness he's accrued from missing his morning nap. He squirms and squeals, so back to the door they go, mom and baby—one united organism of shared genes, dependence, and affection.

For a moment, I forget about them because I am a mother still insulated from the cries of her unborn infant. I do not relate, yet, to the experiences of that young woman (outside? in the bathroom?) trying to come to terms with her disrupted existence. Then there she is, this time looking drained, the slightest exhalation escaping as she attempts to pick up where they left off a few moments earlier. But sometimes the stares aren't all affirming; sometimes those who cluck and coo can suddenly be put off by the ruckus of this baby and his mother, united now by hunger, weariness, and frustration. I see that it is difficult bringing children to church, the way I notice there's a new alto singing in the choir. It registers in a removed and non-urgent sort of way. But my time will come. Yes, indeed . . . my time is coming quickly.

"Mrs. Maddex, I have something I'd like to talk to you about . . . privately." Not knowing what to expect, my concerned mother followed my Sunday school teacher out into the hallway. It was 1978. I had just spent a week with my grandparents in Ohio. My grandfather, Bob, was a surly man with leathery skin and a virtual carpet of salt-and-pepper-colored hair on his head, on his chest, and on his arms. He loved us kids, in a rough-and-tumble kind of way, using terms of affection like "Snake Face" and "Little Ratchet." He captivated our attention with outlandish tales, including one about "the ladies of the night," who would wander the streets of Springfield, whacking unsuspecting pedestrians on the head and then stealing their money.

As soon as it got dark, he'd start with the warnings. "Be careful," he'd say to anyone running out to the store or going for a leisurely stroll through the neighborhood, "Don't let the ladies of the night getcha!" Sometimes, from the porch swing, he would point into darkened alleys, into corners too far to see clearly. "There!" Grandpa would whisper. "Do you see them?" And I did, I swear to you; I wanted to see them and I did.

Back home again, the next Sunday, we went to the Bible church my parents were members of. The lesson in my Sunday school class was on fear, on how God could keep us safe from the common concerns that plague preschoolers. Gathered in a circle, each child took turns admitting their phobias: the dark, dogs, thunder. Then I volunteered, shaking up the boring, "same old, same old," answers with: "I am afraid of the ladies of the night." This response not only rendered my teacher speechless but also sparked the imaginations of my classmates, who would later ask their parents to shed light on this frightening phenomenon. I added, "My grandpa takes me to see them all the time."

As a child, almost everything I knew about God—including His ability to deliver us from our anxieties—I learned from Sunday school, children's church, and Bible camp. My parents fleshed out these lessons effectively, but the majority of my spiritual education was handled solely in age-grouped classrooms (beginning with a nursery for infants and toddlers) by oft-times overwhelmed volunteers who were, nevertheless, dedicated to our spiritual development.

The experience my mom and dad had in church was vastly different from my own. We were on parallel paths that rarely intersected, save for the opening hymn and litany of announcements that commenced the adult service each Sunday. After these were delivered, my brother and I (with great relief) would file out down the aisle to our respective classes. This was ideal, because small children could be antsy, preventing parents from focusing on the words of their pastor. And kids needed a youth-geared approach, including flannel graphs, songs with hand motions, and Scripture quizzes to keep their attention. This was the angle I had always taken. And this was the same angle that would make adjusting to Orthodoxy so very difficult.

The first couple of weeks were dreamy. Elijah slept soundly in the car seat at my feet. Everyone was so congratulatory, and I loved getting out of the house to go to church. I loved taking him up for communion, cradling his chin in my hand as the delicate gold spoon, pressed up against heart-shaped lips, served an infant-sized portion of Christ to my son. It was all so novel; I was married, I was Orthodox, I had a child.

But when Elijah woke up, a few Sundays later, a wave of insecurity swept over me—one that would dampen my liturgical experience for nearly half a decade. I tried to bounce him confidently when he squeaked and squirmed, I tried to look unflustered by his fidgeting. But the truth was, I felt totally inept. So I came and went, like an extra in a musical—off stage, on stage, changing my tune with each new entrance. It felt unfair, me being sequestered in a bathroom stall with my nursing son while everybody else worshipped earnestly, reverently, and in peace—yet I, too, smiled upon my return. "I'm doing just fine as a mother," my facial gesture communicated, but beneath the surface a gnawing dissatisfaction troubled me greatly.

In the fifth grade, I watched a twelve-year-old prodigy from the local junior high school play a breathtaking rendition of "Flight of the Bumble Bee" on her violin. I was mesmerized by the agility of her bow as it raced across the strings. I was captivated by the look of concentration on her face. I was enamored with the sound, intricate and delicate as lace, produced by that instrument in the hands of one so knowledgeable and experienced. That evening, I assured my parents there was nothing else in this world I desired more than violin lessons. I promised them I would practice with the utmost diligence.

When the violin finally arrived, I stroked the burgundy velvet within its case. I painstakingly applied rosin to its bow. I held it under my chin and imagined what I would look like, sound like, and feel like as a violinist. Walking tall, I carried my instrument to that very first practice, where I anticipated a great deal of music-making. But there would be no sounds at all that day except dull explanations on caretaking, vocabulary, and technique. And the lessons that followed were no more stimulating than the first. I played squeaky scales *ad nauseam*, all the while losing my initial passion to the rigors of hard work and repetition. I was disappointed to discover that skills and confidence were not handed out like candy at a Fourth of July parade. It was sobering to get a taste of the effort required to master anything truly exceptional, to make progress one arduous and tiny step at a time.

Have you ever noticed how desperate we are as mothers, working feverishly, hopelessly, to turn our children into an ever-elusive prototype engineered by experts competing for our loyalty? With all of our parenting classes, how-to books, magazines, and department stores, you'd think we'd have it down to a science. And yet, as a whole, we seem more anxious, unconfident, and discontented than our own parents, or their parents before them.

When Elijah showed, early on, signs of being what was once called "strong-willed" (now, I believe, the term "spirited" is more acceptable) I panicked over what I considered to be embarrassing and faulty behavior. He screamed when denied his way and thus he must be fixed, like an aggressive puppy having to learn not to jump up on strangers. So I read and I Googled, I weighed the suggestions to spank, not spank, distract, or empathize. I obsessed and I fretted over what I was doing wrong, because something had to be wrong with a two-year-old boy who refused to be silent or compliant. I had wanted, more than anything else in this world, to be a mother, but it was sobering to discover that skills and confidence could not be bought in the checkout line of a bookstore. It was unnerving to find out that parenting required an awful lot of hard work, setbacks, and faith.

Have you noticed how desperate mothers have become for large blocks of time away from their children? We work, even when we don't have to, because the thought of being home all day long with our toddlers and preschoolers is overwhelming. We hire nannies, spend a fortune on "small tot" music, dance, and soccer programs, and enroll our two-year-olds in pre-preschool classes to give them a leg up on the competition. Because the more our children demand from us, the more doggedly they assert their blossoming wills, the more we resent our lack of freedom; we feel a need to escape in order to preserve our "pre-mommy" identities.

But the more often we escape, the less confident we become in our ability to mother the little people in our care, and thus the fewer connections we are able to make with our families. I hate to admit that in 1999 there were times I, too, wanted to run from Elijah. Before he was born, I could go out to eat, see a movie, stop in at the grocery store, take an impromptu nap, blend in at church, and then, BAM! it was gone, all of it, with a single push that brought my son into this world— into my life. I was gasping for air in an ever-swelling sea of responsibility.

Disappointment continues to catch me off guard no matter how many thousands of times I've felt its pinch. It shouldn't still surprise me that the most anticipated events in my life have almost always been followed by a period of letdown. This was true of vacations, the receiving of coveted gifts, birthday parties, dates, performances, and yes, my conversion to Orthodoxy, and motherhood (the two now intertwined for me into one inseparable knot). And it isn't, I believe, the events themselves that leave me wallowing in a rather vague state of frustration, but rather the inflated expectations I place upon them. That longing for something better, just around the corner, would prove over time to thwart many of my opportunities for spiritual and emotional development.

I remember clearly the first time I felt truly dissatisfied, as if all my ambitions were being suffocated by the mundane-ness of adult responsibilities. I was making numerous copies on the seventh floor of a trucking company. The repetition of blank paper being fed through a machine only to be spit right back out again as a duplicate of the one before it felt a little too close to home. My days were bleeding into one another without distinction—hours of my existence being wasted on a job for which I cared little, for which I was painfully, mad-deningly ill suited.

For a while there, things looked promising; professors had been encouraging about my prospects as an impetus for change, school-free independence had been an exhilarating achievement, and the marriage I had recently entered into proved to be a titillating venture fraught with both passion and insecurity. But one cannot keep up forever with that feverish pace. I suspect that Visa bills and ten-hour workdays have leveled many a high hope, tempered plenty of idealistic aspirations. At the time, however, while Xeroxing my life away, that natural progression towards maturation felt more like "selling out"; waiting for something else to come along was nearly unbearable.

News of my pregnancy was a light at the end of the tunnel. I would find clarity in motherhood. I would devote myself to the ecstasy of becoming a cocreator. I would lose myself in the gratification of raising children. The eight-month countdown to my last day as a corporate communications administrative assistant I viewed as a period of incubation. Every thought and action was devoted to a future starting point. Every day was another square to check off my calendar until real life, my more meaningful life, would begin. And when, at last, I had trudged through all those peripheral moments leading up to the afternoon of my son's birth, I delighted in the newfound freedom to let go of old expectations and embrace the sacrificial persona of caregiver, nurturer, and parent.

I poured out that optimism into my perfectly beautiful infant, who instinctively sucked every last bit of it from my sleep-deprived, overwhelmed, and lonely soul. And when the well was dry, when the weeks had turned into months without removing from me permanently the hunger for something more, the discontentment I couldn't shake no matter how hard I prayed, wished, or manipulated my circumstances—I finally stopped trying altogether. It turns out I liked the idea of liberation (from boredom, my sins, the less-than-perfect circumstances in which I often found myself) much more than the reality of what that said deliverance required.

I was right about Orthodoxy and motherhood being

more than capable of stripping away my tendencies toward self-centeredness, but naïve to imagine that such a process would be, for the most part, pleasant and perhaps even thrilling. After the honeymoon phase of birth and conversion, the permanency of what I had entered into—long services, long nights, a steady string of stringent demands upon my time, patience, and confidence—sank in like a swallowed boulder: all weighty, obvious, and intrusive. It turned out that authentic freedom (from the bondage of pouring all my effort into the slippery, bottomless, and hopelessly nebulous pit of my misguided assumptions) required a good old-fashioned demolition of my old self in order to rebuild a brand new self, hollowed out and open wide for Christ's presence.

Imagine how elated the Israelites must have felt, after years of captivity and backbreaking labor, to walk triumphantly out of Egypt as free men and women—to watch their children rejoice in the defeat of their oppressors. I wonder how long they continued their cries of thanksgiving, how many days the jubilation stayed its course, before gratitude gave way to resentment as the miles stretched on endlessly and their sustenance of manna, consistently provided from the hand of God, lost its novelty. How long did it take (weeks? months? years?) for the bulk of them to forget completely about the Promised Land, the miraculous intervention of Moses and his treasure trove of plagues, their bloodied doorways signaling death would not be entering because the almighty God was on their side? What was the final impetus for not only losing hope but for actively and unapologetically turning their backs on their one true Savior in exchange for a material god of their own design? I'd be the first to "tsk, tsk" such flagrant heresy if I weren't so darned guilty of those exact same transgressions—if I myself could remember to hold out for, and surrender my faulty desires to, Christ's promises.

Yes, I was disappointed—that having a baby wasn't all cuddles and warm tingling fulfillment; that a consistent hunger for prayer, confession, and two-hour feastday services wasn't an automatic component of chrismation; that a nursery wasn't available for Elijah when he was fussy and I was desperate for just a little bit of quiet to worship attentively; and that wandering awhile through the wilderness was a mandatory precursor to finding my way Home.

The Lord said: "He who endures patiently to the end will be saved" (Mt. 10:22). Patient endurance is the consolidation of all the virtues, because without it not one of them can subsist. For whoever turns back is not "fit for the kingdom of heaven" (Luke 9:62). Indeed, even though someone thinks that he is in possession of all the virtues, he is still not fit for the kingdom until he has first endured to the end and escaped from the snares of the devil; for only thus can he attain it. Even those who have received a foretaste of the kingdom stand in need of patient endurance if they are to gain their final reward in the age to be. Indeed, in every form of learning and knowledge persistence is needed. This is natural, since even sensible things cannot be produced without it: when any such thing is born, there has to be a period of patient waiting if it is to continue to live. (St. Peter of Damascus, Philokalia, Faber & Faber, Vol. 3)

Patient endurance—oh my, what a concept, in a land of "Give me everything, and I mean now!" It would naturally take awhile to adjust my calcified view of salvation from instant completion to a more gradual and consistent sacrifice of my best-laid plans and presumptions. Orthodoxy and motherhood were not going to be the "extreme makeovers" I originally envisioned, improving my character through a series of quick, Christ-performed nips and tucks while I lay motionless and unresponsive on the table. On the contrary, I was in training for a marathon—pushing myself every day to bear the soreness for just a little bit longer, refueling my weary spirit with the Eucharist, shedding the superfluous weight of pride and egotism through discipline and endurance. Only through a dedicated cooperation on my part with Christ's eternal and unknowable plan would I be strengthened.

So while it seemed that I was a bit lost, groping my way through motherhood and staring awestruck into the expansiveness of the Orthodox Faith, I retained my strong belief that there was nothing more worthwhile than immersing myself in both of them. I was, in fact, exactly where I ought to be—at the starting gate of the only race that mattered.

Chapter Seven

Comparisons

I doubted highly that the other mothers and caretakers would be conscientious enough to pack non-hydrogenated protein bars and an all-natural sports drink in their child's gym bag. But to be fair, our Chicago neighborhood was considered low-income, and thus most moms didn't have the option to stay home full-time, homeschool, and shop at organic grocery stores. "Oh well," I sighed, "this will be a good opportunity for Elijah to socialize, get some exercise, and provide a good example to his fellow six-year-old participants in the local park district tumbling class."

He seemed excited enough as we pulled into the parking lot. "Stay by the van," I ordered, while unbuckling four-year-old Priscilla and two-year-old Ben from their car seats. We were running a tad late, so I rushed us through the doorway; the smells of sweat and shoe leather only heightened our anticipation.

"Do you want me to stay around?" I called after Elijah, who, ever true to his character, was already stretching, conversing, and embracing this novel experience.

"If you want!" he yelled back, obviously unconcerned over my decision whether to watch him in action or go home. So I waved goodbye, promising to be back in an hour and a half; it felt good to get a break while Elijah flipped, balanced, and somersaulted—while he frolicked in his newfound independence. Yes, this tumbling class would be a win-win situation for both of us.

I arrived back about fifteen minutes early, smiling amiably at the staff, the instructors, the other parents picking up and dropping off their children. Priscilla and Benjamin sat wide-eyed against the wall of the gymnasium. Elijah and his peers lined up for the final activity—an obstacle course involving floor mats, balance beam, and uneven bars.

Miss Stacey was explaining the rules when Elijah started poking at the boy in front of him. "Stop it," the boy growled, but Elijah kept at it, oblivious to the frustration he was evoking not only in his classmate, but in his teacher as well.

"I need everyone's eyes and ears on me, please!" she shouted for what I can only imagine was the fiftieth time in the last ninety minutes.

"Elijah!" I loudly whispered in an effort to distract him. "Be sure you listen to the teacher and get in line, okay?"

Once back in the van I peppered him with questions.

"How was class?"

"Fine."

"Was your teacher nice?"

"Yeah."

"What was your favorite part?"

"Snack. Mom?"

"Yes, sweetheart?"

"I don't want to go back."

My next series of maniacal questions ("Why not?" "What's wrong?" "Are you too tired?" "Were the other kids mean?" "Was the gym really hot?") went mostly unanswered, although I did pull out of him his dislike for the stretch where you sit down and hold your ankles together while flapping your knees like a butterfly.

After talking with my calm and rational husband, I decided that Elijah just wasn't used to a structured environment. He needed to stick with the class and learn how to follow rules, pay attention, and be part of a group with an authority figure other than his mother.

The second day he acted fine, and I didn't waste my breath on overly intrusive questions. When I went to pick him up the third day, however, Elijah was separated from the other kids with his head down, looking sad and deflated. I entered the gym as the teacher put her arm around him and kindly nudged him toward me.

"Do you want to tell your mom what happened today?"

Silence.

"Elijah, why did you have to sit out away from the rest of the class?"

Unbearable silence.

Most of the caregivers had arrived by then to pick up their kids, none of them (besides myself) having to make excuses for their behavior. All eyes were on Miss Stacey, Elijah, and me.

"Elijah is having a hard time following instructions," his teacher began. "When we sit down for stretching, he won't participate because he says his stomach hurts. I let him lie on the mat, but he won't stay there either. As soon as we start a relay race or an obstacle course he wants to join in again, but has a difficult time waiting his turn. He is a sweet boy, Mrs. Sabourin, but I have a large class here and I can't afford to spend the majority of my time working with just one child."

I assured Miss Stacey in my calmest mommy voice that I completely understood. My husband and I would certainly talk with Elijah and make sure he recognized the importance of being a cooperative member of her group. She smiled, relieved, and gave Elijah a big hug.

At home that evening I racked my brain for a possible solution to our gymnastics class dilemma. I wanted to teach Elijah how to take ownership of his actions without shaming him into withdrawing completely. I came up with four typed questions on a sheet of paper:

Did Elijah participate in all activities?

Did Elijah wait his turn in line?

Did Elijah interrupt Miss Stacey?

Did Elijah follow instructions?

After reading them to my son and making sure he had a solid understanding of what his teacher, father, and I expected, I explained that he would bring that form to every class, and when I picked him up afterwards, he, Miss Stacey, and I would all go over it together. There would be a reward if the answers to all four questions were favorable.

The next day, Elijah and I presented our plan to his teacher. I could tell she was impressed and very pleased that I was taking such an active role in the situation. Miss Stacey was enthusiastic about participating, and I allowed myself to feel pride and fulfillment in a job well done. I hadn't panicked or given up on Elijah's ability to grow and mature; I had found a solution that he and I both could understand, and had found in Miss Stacey another adult to reinforce the positive social behavior I so desperately wanted to instill in my children.

The next three hours dragged on. I was anxious to hear how much progress Elijah had made. I didn't expect perfection, by any means, but I was definitely hoping for something, anything to validate my efforts.

The scene I came back to made my heart sink. Miss Stacey's eyes expressed everything I didn't want to hear before she even opened her mouth. Elijah had basically repeated the same behavior from the day before and seemed to care little about the questions, Miss Stacey's answers, or the promised reward.

"Maybe he isn't quite ready for this," she suggested. I nodded, grabbed his hand and sports bottle, and threw all of us in the van. As soon as the door shut, my eyes were wet and my teeth clenched. In the rearview mirror I could see Elijah laughing with his brother and sister, completely unaware of the anger and embarrassment I was scarcely containing.

"Mommy," he asked lightheartedly, "when we get home can I have a Popsicle?"

"No, Elijah! I am very frustrated with you right now! You will not get any treats and you will not be getting any computer or TV time either. Why didn't you listen? Why couldn't you participate like the other kids in your class?"

"I don't know. Can I have a Popsicle tomorrow?"

The tears began streaming; my thoughts turned brutal, fragmented, and irrational. I was furious at Elijah for making me look inadequate, for having a short attention span, for being cavalier about his shortcomings, and for not living up to my ideals.

Of the many cracks in my mothering armor, there is one that leaves my children and me particularly vulnerable to harm: a subconscious habit of judging my family in regard to how we measure up to others. I am ashamed to admit how many years I wasted trying to be somebody I wasn't, or how many M&M's I consumed because our papers were chronically out of order, the clutter more conniving than my impractical cleaning schedule, or because the laundry had been washed with a tube of greasy Chapstick in my pants pocket . . . again.

I got downright crabby when my idealized self stood just inches out of reach, looking more muscular, organized, and outgoing than this all-too-human flabby-thighed mother pressing her nose against the glass that divided heavily marketed pipe dreams from reality. My neck was chronically sore from craning over fences for a nice long look at where the grass was always greener, the children better behaved, and scrapbooks filled to overflowing with anecdotes and updated photographs. Guess how few people were blessed by my neurotic desire for flawlessness?

It started when Elijah was a toddler, in church of all places, with a little boy his age who sat quietly near his parents during Liturgy. I just couldn't get it—why my kid insisted on whining and wriggling away from my grip while this well-groomed toddler several feet in front of us could flip contentedly through a children's book about the saints. Every week it was the same: me grimacing through an hour of whispered scolding and frequent trips to the parking lot so that Elijah could run a bit and hopefully work off some of that pent-up energy.

I'd return to join the other moms who hadn't left the service, whose own small children were either propped contentedly on their hips or fiddling inconspicuously with their shoelaces on the floor in front of them. "Please," I silently begged Elijah, the son I both adored and feared for his intensity, active imagination, and fierce dependence on me, his refuge, his world, his mother: "just once, could you let me get through a Sunday without feeling like such a failure?"

I tried to heed the advice so readily offered by well-intentioned parishioners who could see and hear me struggling to get control.

"Don't let him out of your arms."

"Walk him around and let him see the candles and the icons up close."

"Bring him to more services so he'll get used to it."

"Bring him to fewer services so he won't resent them."

"Put a small blanket on the floor and tell him he can't move off of it until the Liturgy is over."

Nothing made a difference save the months that passed imperceptibly by. Elijah's vocabulary increased, decreasing his need to break down in frustration when I couldn't understand what he wanted. His growing body eventually required only one nap instead of two. He was adjusting and developing within his own distinct time frame—a time frame, quite naturally, unlike anybody else's.

Looking back, I can see how impossible I was to satisfy. Being a first-time mother, I worried about everything, and I do mean every possible stupid thing you can imagine. If Elijah had been shy and quiet, I would have pushed him to be more outgoing; I would have lain awake at night wondering what I had done to squelch his confidence. I would have seen another child talking effortlessly, even too loudly (much to his own mother's chagrin), to children and adults alike and would have felt guilty for wishing my child didn't cling to my leg so.

And I was no easier on myself—assessing my piety, my attire, my maternal capabilities in light of other women, some of whom (along with their young families) attended every service scheduled, ground their own wheat to make bread, and raised kids who, in my own self-degrading imagination, delighted in and thrived on every single aspect of Orthodoxy.

We all have our individual strengths and weaknesses, and yet as mothers it is all too easy to despise our uniqueness rather than relish it. When I am working extra hard, let's say, on keeping my kids on a predictable schedule, I will inevitably run into a mom working extra hard on getting her kids out of a rut and into more cultural experiences, like museums and art classes. Instead of saying, "Good for her, her children will appreciate that," my tendency is to turn inward and compare myself on an ever-sliding scale that will always make her look better and me feel worse.

In fact, no matter how hard I try, there will always be women who cook better, have more patience, weigh less, are more educated, and have cleaner homes than I. A dear friend of mine once admitted during a particularly stressful time in her life that she would tell herself, when a guest in someone else's house, that their bathroom was clean only because they knew she was coming; otherwise she would feel too down about her own dirty bathroom waiting for her at home.

Although it seems like a rather negative approach, I eventually found great relief from such pessimism and unproductive thinking by accepting the cold hard truth that I will never be perfect. I am a wonderfully flawed human being, and any kind of sweeping and lofty goal will result in me falling flat on my face one hundred percent of the time. The minute I decide to no longer lose my temper (not eat sugar, exercise seven days a week, pray without ceasing—just fill in whatever applies), I aim for a total annihilation of a particular bad habit with all the sleep-deprived, stretched-thin strength I can muster. When that proves to be insufficient for the task at hand, it is never a small slip-up but a full-scale catastrophe in the form of a yelling frenzy, a consumed bag of chocolate chips, or a mildewed load of forgotten laundry in the washer.

When I put before me a goal as elusive as perfection, my days are wasted on depression and self-criticism. More than an organized closet, more than my being ten pounds lighter, more than being enrolled in the coolest extracurricular activities, certainly more than homemade bread, my family wants my time, gentleness, and serenity. I have one, two, three, four kids who are happiest when I am contented, with the idiosyncrasies that make me as irreplaceable as a well-worn rag doll adored for her ability to take a lickin' and keep on givin' much-needed affection, warmth, and security. I have a husband who would like to be heard, the kind of hearing where you put down the broom, the dishrag, or the magazine in order to look at a person square in the face with attention. I am a vital component of Christ's Church, where the diversity among its members is necessary for sustained health and survival; a spine and thousands of identical right arms do not a functioning body make.

I could try to be you, all clever and crafty and virtuous, or her with the delicately feminine disposition; but eventually my real, Molly Ann Sabourin self would rip holes all through that disingenuous disguise. It is my first fruits God is asking of me—my talents, my quirky habits and convictions. It would be awfully counterproductive to try to work out my own salvation with fear and trembling by concentrating on everybody else's.

I know I am impatient. I know I am absent-minded. I know I struggle with being too impulsive and easily distracted. I know I am selfish, but I also know that I am the very best mom for the wonderfully human kids God gave me. If I start each day with a prayer of humility, admitting that on my own I will really mess things up, my mind and heart remain open for help and direction. I set tiny goals, like not yelling through breakfast, or putting aside my "work" to sit and play one game of the children's choice.

When my kids see my vulnerabilities, when they hear

me apologize if I have wronged them, they are always loving and accepting of my blunders. When I expect too much of myself, however, pushing all of us too hard in the process, they become hurt, discouraged, and resentful. Each morning we are given the incredible opportunity to start over. Every day we get a new chance to be kinder, calmer, and more aware of the quiet needs surrounding us. Imagine how fulfilling it would be if we took our eyes off the status quo and listened with interest to the dreams, fears, and laughter of our children.

Here is the analogy that pops into my head when I think of the way I often mother versus the way I wish I could mother all the time. The way I often mother is like a high school senior being taught home economics by an instructor who has presented her class with a very nice cake. A recipe has been handed out to each of us with specific instructions on how we, in turn, can create its exact replica. We will be graded, in fact, on how similar our cakes turn out to be in taste, texture, and appearance. Our instructor tells us what ingredients to use, and in what order they should be added. She then tells us how to stir, sift, and pour the mixture into our baking pans. Meanwhile, we keep a close eye on the students to our right and left: "Are they dropping eggshells in the mixing bowl? Is their batter too lumpy?" Finally, we stick our projects in the oven while holding our collective breath, hoping the directions were foolproof and that our cakes will turn out well, based on the expertise of others.

The way I wish I could mother all the time is like a great chef. A truly great chef is not tied to a recipe but rather pays careful attention to her instincts, knowing by her love and familiarity for the foods with which she is working whether a dish needs to be simmered, boiled, or cooled off completely. She has learned through trial and error that because the materials she creates with are fresh, they often behave in ways unexpected. To account for this she alters the amount of spices added until they enhance without overpowering the final product; the result is flavorful, distinctive, and satisfying. And finally, after pouring into it all her heart, intuition, and respect, she revels in offering that meal so painstakingly prepared as a delight and nourishment to others.

When I catch Elijah's eye during Liturgy, I smile warmly, but he doesn't so much as wink or nod back at me in return. You see, he serves behind the altar now, and takes that responsibility very seriously. Some Sundays I'm too busy chasing down his younger sister Mary to pause and reflect on the magnitude of this recent development. But other times I am acutely, even tearfully, aware of its significance.

I'd be lying if I said the years between the chaos and eventual control passed by in a heartbeat. Every stage Elijah enters and exits is more vivid and intense than those I will sprint through with his siblings. He is my firstborn, my initiation into every new experience I must process as a mother; we have grown up side by side in many ways. This is what I think about when he walks out ahead of our priest for the Great Entrance, candle in hand: how we inched our way here, too often encumbered by my own misconceptions.

I have, admittedly, lost a lot of pride along the way. But what I've gained is a longer fuse, a more urgent dependence on Christ, and a deep-seated appreciation for the temperaments, talents, and blemishes that make each member of my family undeniably precious and exceptional. I pray daily for the strength to love each of my children for who and what they are as individuals—my blessings, my joy, my salvation.

Chapter Eight

Acceptance

I bolt upright in bed at the sound of my phone ringing; it's five-thirty A.M. Expectantly, I run into the kitchen to answer it. I have been waiting for this call for a week. One of my dearest friends in the world is about to have a baby.

I met Jennifer when I was nineteen years old. She was, and still is, creative, intelligent, attentive, and wickedly funny. I knew from the start we would be great friends. After graduating from college, Jennifer began her career as a product buyer for a bookstore in downtown Chicago. She was good at her job and loved being part of the city. In 2000 she met, fell in love with, got engaged to, and married her husband Nathan. I gave the toast at her wedding and meant every warm sentiment I nervously offered. It was a marriage to which you could feel good about raising your glass. Within the year, Jennifer was pregnant.

Although the pregnancy was a surprise, Jennifer warmed up to the idea of being a mother relatively quickly. By the time she made the mental shift, however, her body had taken on a mind of its own. Her nausea was at times debilitating.

Indigestion forced her to sleep sitting up, and she found it impossible to limit her weight gain to the doctor's recommended twenty-five pounds. She was surprised by the guilt, fear, and frustration she was battling on a daily basis. She felt resentful about losing control of her figure and then guilty for her vanity. She felt angry at being sick and then disturbed by her ungratefulness. The messages Jennifer received from friends, doctors, family, and the media were both conflicted and convoluted.

At the end of her first trimester, Jennifer and Nathan went to her prenatal visit hoping to get some relief from her lingering morning sickness. They were expecting some vitamin supplements, a prescription, or, at the very least, some "this too shall pass" encouragement. Her assigned physician was out of the office, so she and Nathan met with a different doctor in the practice who, to their horror, asked simply whether they wanted to continue with the pregnancy. Needless to say, Jen and Nathan were speechless. What they wanted was a supportive push over the first of the many difficult hurdles they would soon encounter. What they got was a flippant and irresponsible "if you can't take the heat, get out of the kitchen" slap in the face.

After nine long months (during the last of which she could wear no shoes but a pair of black-and-gray flip-flops she had picked up at a gas station), Jennifer's water broke and labor began. If her pregnancy had been an uphill climb to the mountain of motherhood, then her birth experience was a thunderous avalanche. When Jen arrived at the hospital, labor was induced, which brought on painful contractions—one on top of the other. She was given an epidural for the pain, but her labor was not progressing and the baby's heart rate was slowing down. Before she knew it, her room was filled with concerned-looking doctors and nurses suggesting an emergency C-section "right this minute." She and Nathan were exhausted when their beautiful baby boy finally emerged from Jen's scarred and tender belly. Owen was sent to the intensive care unit for observation, and Jennifer was sent to her room to rest.

Since Jennifer's job provided the couple's health insurance, they had decided before Owen was born that she would go back to work after her six-week maternity leave. "That will be plenty of time," she thought, "to bond with the baby, physically heal from the birth, and get breastfeeding underway."

Never in her detailed plan did she schedule in the hazy postpartum fog that was awaiting her. Trying for hours to push out a baby, only to be then cut open and stitched back up, can do a real number on an already overtaxed postpartum body. Jennifer really wanted to breastfeed, but Owen was given bottles whenever he felt hungry in the ICU and wasn't interested in learning new feeding tricks three days later. In an effort to keep up her milk supply, Jennifer pumped every two hours, freezing her milk and giving it to Owen in the bottles to which he had grown accustomed. Her apartment was filled with tiny diapers, stress, and the hum of a breast pump slowly sucking the life from her.

The schedule was brutal and sleep was scarce. She wanted to give up and switch to formula, but each setback represented for her yet another reason to see herself as a horrible mother. Her body had failed her in pregnancy and then again in birth. She lacked the stamina to endure the pain of scabbed nipples and a tiny infant wailing and writhing with hunger. She could not stop crying during what should have been the happiest and most meaningful moments of her life. Her husband was confused and, quite frankly, terrified by his scraggly-haired, topless, swollen and irrational wife.

When those six weeks came to an end, Jennifer could not

imagine putting her tiny son into daycare and going back to work full-time. Nathan was anxious to take care of Jennifer's needs, so the two of them, with the support of flexible supervisors, worked out a plan in which she would work three days from home and two days in the office. Nathan would do the opposite, making day care unnecessary. This was the plan to which they stuck for the next two years. Her bookstore was then bought out, and she was given the choice either to stay and work full-time or to be unemployed. Jennifer's job paid more than Nathan's and had better benefits. She felt she just had to work.

Having a fulfilling job invigorated Jennifer. She loved the feedback, the conversation, putting on lipstick, and leaving the house. But working full-time was quickly testing her resolve to juggle so many roles at once. Owen became very attached to Nathan, often pushing Jennifer away when she came home. It would take a whole weekend for Owen to warm up to her, and then she was back at work Monday morning, the routine starting all over again. Jennifer wanted desperately to be the center of her son's life. His little cold shoulder chipped away at her heart, turning her sadness into anger.

After one year of that hectic schedule, Jennifer knew something major had to change. The part-time job at which Nathan had been working from home was available full-time, but the couple would have to leave Chicago to make it work on one income. Jennifer gave her two-weeks' notice, packed up the apartment, and left the city she had called home for the past ten years.

"I thought staying home full-time would be easy," she told me. "No deadlines, more time on my hands to work on the house, get in better shape physically. I am a woman," she figured. "Mothering will be instinctive."

At work, Jennifer's calendar told her what to do, when to do it, and how long each task should take. "What was most surprising," she now says, "was how long the days seemed to be." Owen needed so much of her attention. Everything from washing the dishes to going to the grocery store took an enormous amount of time. Once again, resentment reared its ugly head when she couldn't get everything done. She actually gained weight because she was no longer walking the Chicago streets to get to work, lunch, or the parking lot. The pace was slow and the work often "fruitless"; the to-do list was always taunting her. It took a long time for Jen to untangle herself from her pre-mommy expectations and adapt to a broader definition of "productive."

It remains a daily struggle. "I had no idea how selfish I could be. It is still hard for me to stop what I am working on and really listen to what Owen needs."

Not too long ago we were reminiscing about those difficult weeks after Owen's birth and reflecting on our current challenge not to wish away the frustrations linked inseparably to the thrills and unearthly satisfaction that come with raising our children. "You know what?" she asked. "There is so much I wish someone had candidly told me about motherhood. Somebody should write a really honest book about it."

"Exactly," I thought. "Exactly."

When it's freezing outside and money is scarce, we hit the library. One day, three of us—my sister-in-law, Paige, our friend Kris, and I—huddled around a child-sized table piled messily with stickers, crayons, and paper. It was unusually crowded, unusually noisy. Static-haired kids ran largely unsupervised while their moms flipped through magazines and occasionally tossed out verbal reprimands for particularly aggressive behavior. "Share, please, Ethan. No running, Lucy."

Admittedly, I too kept a distant eye on my own rowdy charges, so interesting to me was the conversation at hand. Kris had been reading a book about a woman who claimed she had "found herself" by way of a divorce and some global traveling. Depression had been oppressing her, making more and more obvious her discontentment with marriage and the overall life she was immersed in. Courageously, she cut the ties that were binding her to an unsatisfactory existence and became proactive in achieving her own sense of worth and fulfillment.

Her story has inspired women everywhere to step up and reclaim their dreams—desires too often smothered by busyness and responsibility. I understand why the author of this very popular memoir has been embraced with open arms by the overworked and underappreciated masses, because I, too, tend to burn with motivation when self-help cheerleaders spread their "the sky is the limit" mantra. "I am more than this!" I begin thinking to myself, which is accurate but also tricky. How I interpret that statement is of utmost importance, lest I sprint around in circles chasing hopes that pop like bubbles once you touch them.

Like Jennifer, I also fight daily to accept the inconveniences of motherhood. Every morning I awake to very visible, audible, unignorable boundaries. My role as a stay-at-home mother limits quite severely any opportunities for being recognized as something other than an enforcer of rules, a provider of meals, a stereotype of societal irrelevance. There are days I am fine with this, I can take it all in stride—the demands, repetition, lack of praise—until, that is, a longing to be referred to by my given name (as opposed to "Mommy, can I . . . ?") swells so suddenly within me I fear I'll crack in two from all the strain. I try to spare myself the guilt of treating such a reflexive impulse as sinful, ungrateful, or selfish; I have no more control over these periodic flare-ups than I do over hunger or fatigue. It is the crucial minutes following, when I decide what to do or where to go with the restlessness, that reveal everything.

If there were a way to live effectively for Christ and for your own happiness, I for sure would have found it by now. The number of man-hours I've spent testing that possibility makes me pretty much an expert in the field of wishy-washyness, so please, just trust me on this one. What never works, upon reaching the end of oneself, is stoking outlandish "what-ifs" until the fantasy of a better job, a better spouse, a better income becomes in your mind the only viable option for relief from the constriction of your current circumstances.

What I've been known to do is to mix a little bit of faith with a whole lot of assumptions about what would be best for me at any given moment. I'd toss out a prayer for guidance boomerang-style, letting go of my self-will for just a second before reaching right out to grab it back again. "Here's what I propose; please make it happen. Amen." From there I would either force a change, in the name of God, or question His goodness when my best-laid plans fell through. Either way, I missed the point entirely. I lost my sense of direction by running both to Jesus and from Him simultaneously.

It is through my Orthodox faith that I am learning to be still, and that is no small statement considering my propensity to wander. In this apostolic Church, sacraments and liturgy can—through real, not merely symbolic, miracles—tame a girl's obsession with herself, unraveling completely the surprisingly ineffectual theory that being catered to, entertained, released from trials, brings satisfaction. It turns out

that the receiving of holy chrism at one's baptism or chrismation, the regular partaking of the actual Body and Blood of
Christ, absolution through confession, and joining with martyrs and saints in the worship of the Holy Trinity can transform an individual from within. Such established Traditions
take into account that I am human and weak and foolish.
These enduring and consecrated gifts have overridden my
faulty preferences, and after ten years' time are finally pen-
etrating my thick soul with the only truth that matters: I *am*
more than this—in that I, we, were created to serve, praise,
be filled with Christ Jesus.

Every day, before facing a new morning guaranteed to be
filled with challenges and uncertainty, I plead in the prayer of
Metropolitan Philaret:

> *O Lord, give me the strength to greet the coming day in peace.*
> *Help me in all things to rely on Your holy will. Reveal Your*
> *will to me every hour of the day. Bless my dealings with all peo-*
> *ple. Teach me to treat all people who come to me throughout*
> *the day with peace of soul and with firm conviction that Your*
> *will governs all. In all my deeds and words, guide my thoughts*
> *and feelings. In unexpected events, let me not forget that all are*
> *sent by You. Teach me to act firmly and wisely, without embit-*
> *tering and embarrassing others. Give me the physical strength*
> *to bear the labors of this day. Direct my will; teach me to pray;*
> *pray You Yourself in me. Amen.*

It's nuts around here—I've had four hours of sleep, the children are bickering, no one is pleased about my dinner plans,
and there is a fork in the road, two paths to choose from:
resentment or the illogical thankfulness found only in relation
to the Kingdom of heaven. Spiritually, emotionally, physically
I stay in the thick of it, and find Christ—designing the daily

ups and downs that will most effectively strip me of the longing to be anywhere but in His presence. It's not always pretty, but today I'll take authentic purpose over fleeting glamour, and pray tomorrow for the strength to do the same.

Only when I accept and embrace the dichotomy that through surrendering my life I will gain it does it start to make sense to me why Orthodox Christians can't live by the rules governing secular society. As my friend Ser so aptly put it, in reference to a discussion on the book I refer to above: "What I am learning very, very slowly is that it is not 'I am more than this' but that 'this is so much more than what it seems.'"

There is a reason my life revolves entirely around the Eucharist, like a planet kept in orbit by the sun. I would float into oblivion without the Church to keep me stable, to keep me from burning with unrequited passions or freezing from the bitterness of futility. After years of clawing at the walls of motherhood, I gave up in exhaustion only to find out through confession, Orthodox theology, and unconditional love that the demands of raising young children brought with themselves the potential for spiritual fulfillment and freedom from the unquenchable dissatisfaction of living for myself alone.

I used to wrestle with the verse in 1 Timothy, "Nevertheless [women] will be saved in childbearing if they continue in faith, love, and holiness, with self-control" (2:15). As a liberated female, easily turned off by any semblance of sexism or intolerance, I struggled to find the modern-day significance in such a statement. I had worked hard for my college education. I had plans to become a writer, a teacher, maybe both. Surely God didn't mean for me to throw all that away and lose myself in the breeding of babies! Surely I could, I would, have it all! Isn't that our right? Isn't that our obligation—to prove our equality by juggling family, careers, and ambitions? What was wrong with me, then, when at the prime of my life

I had not one extra ounce of energy to pursue anything other than taking care of my infant son? Why, with all the options available to me for self-improvement, could I only find relief from my agitation in the very verse I originally dismissed as "irrelevant"?

All these tears and years later, I accept that this is the case because children contain within themselves the ability to push us farther and to make us love more deeply than we ever could have managed on our own; because children can drive us crazy one minute and then delight us and fill us with unequivocal joy the next; because our children, perhaps more than any other stimulus, have the capacity to inspire us in our faith.

The question I need to ask myself is not, "What, in addition to the blessings right before me, would make me happier?" It is rather, "What do I need to rid myself of in order not to get sidetracked from my first and foremost goal of achieving salvation?"

"Let us lay aside every weight, and the sin which so easily ensnares us," wrote St. Paul in Hebrews 12:1, "and let us run with endurance the race that is set before us." Just as excess amounts of rich and decadent foods can be addictive and impair our ability to sense fullness, our craving for worldly pleasures only intensifies the more we stuff ourselves with passions, possessions, and misguided assumptions.

There is a story in William J. Bennett's *The Book of Virtues* called "The Magic Thread," which fascinates both my children and me. It begins with the following introduction:

Too often, people want what they want (or what they think they want, which is usually "happiness" in one form or another) right now. The irony of their impatience is that only by learning to wait, and by a willingness to accept the bad with the good, do we usually attain those things that are truly worthwhile. (The Book of Virtues, *Simon & Schuster, p. 57)*

The story goes on to describe a little boy named Peter who did not like to go to school and was forever distracted by his daydreams. Peter had a hard time living fully in each moment, choosing rather to long for the future, when he'd be all grown up and free from his chores and lessons. One day in the forest he met an elderly woman who offered him a silver ball from which hung a golden thread. "This is your life thread," she told him. "Do not touch it and time will pass normally. But if you wish time to pass more quickly, you only have to pull the thread a little way and an hour will pass like a second. But I warn you, once the thread has been pulled out, it cannot be pushed in again. It will disappear like a puff of smoke."

Peter vowed to use the ball carefully and only for emergencies, but as you can imagine, the temptation was much too enormous to bear. You see, there was a girl he loved, but they were too young to marry. With just a tiny pull of that thread, he was able to wed her immediately. "That's it," he promised, "I will be happy with where I'm at," but then, of course, there were other trials and inconveniences that stood between him and his peace of mind. His baby, whom he adored, would often cry at night, disrupting their sleep. Pull, pull . . . poof! The baby was happy.

When Peter spoke out against corruption in the government, he was sent to prison. Pull, pull . . . poof! He was home again, although now much older—a middle-aged man. There were financial troubles and sick children and his wife, so very tired from her motherly duties. And so he pulled and pulled and pulled that thread, passing over years full of heartache—and possibly joy? Enlightenment? Growth? How would he ever know? Those moments were gone, gone forever.

Suddenly, the extent of the damage done became painfully, frighteningly obvious. Peter's hair was white, his body was frail, and his beloved wife was old now, just as he was. While pondering on these things, he wandered once again into the same forest he used to escape to as a child, and there met the same woman who had given him the magic ball. When she asked if he had enjoyed her gift, he responded, "Your magic ball is a wonderful thing. I have never had to suffer or wait for anything in my life. And yet it all passed so quickly. I feel that I have had no time to take in what has happened to me, neither the good things nor the bad. Now there is so little time left. I dare not pull the thread again, for it will only bring me to my death."

He begged for one final wish. To live his life over, without the magic ball and without the possibility of bypassing the many difficulties his life would surely entail. And yes, as in all good fairy tales, his wish was granted. Peter woke as from a dream, a little boy again with his whole life ahead of him.

Had I my own magic ball, the results would be disastrous, the temptation much too strong for me to handle. It's the little things, those many little annoying things that I'd think nothing about skipping over with a tug on that golden thread. Yesterday, for instance, my day was packed with plans, including a stop at the library. "Grab the books on tape!" I yelled to Elijah on the way to our van, my keys in hand.

"Uh, Mom," he said, "one's missing." And thus began a frustrating and time-consuming search for one lone cassette tape, without which we'd be unable to check out anything new.

The longer we looked, the angrier I became. "What a waste!" I grumbled inwardly, and yet how strange that I was surprised by such a typical interruption to my agenda. I'd even go so far as to say, these scenarios involving my having to wait due to temper tantrums, spills, and lost shoes or keys make up the bulk of my existence as a mother. This won't always be the case, but right now it is. The next stage will have its own share of dilemmas that I'll complain about, and would gladly skip over if I could—which is why, my dear friends, it is so important that we pause to reevaluate our priorities.

If God truly is everywhere present and fills all things, we need not fear that satisfaction cannot be found within our present afflictions, as maddening as they may sometimes be. Let us try, when we reach our breaking point, instead of writhing in desperation for an escape, to quiet our souls and pray, "Lord, have mercy! I am here. I am listening. Please give me strength. Please give me wisdom. Amen."

Let us daydream less and pay attention more by loving, learning, apologizing, sacrificing, forgiving—living, like there's no tomorrow.

Chapter Nine

Isolation

My niece, Isabelle, was only three weeks old when my sister-in-law, Paige, slipped her delicate, wriggly body into a pink and ruffled outfit before buckling her into the baby seat and driving to Austin, Texas, for the wedding of Paige's younger sister. This would be their first real outing since the birth and, wow, what an outing it was! Distant friends and relatives would all be gathered together for a once-in-a-lifetime event—one that Paige had been looking forward to for months.

For Paige, motherhood was, as yet, more of a newly applied label than a reality that had soaked in over time and with practice. Isabelle was precious but unpredictable; her presence at such a lavish celebration was akin to bringing a potty-training toddler, sans a pull-up or diaper, to an art exhibit. It could be mildly hectic but relatively fine, or on the other hand it might turn out to be a messy, embarrassing disaster.

Of course Paige would wear heels to a formal affair, heels and an elegant dress. But the addition of an infant car seat hanging awkwardly from her forearm encumbered severely her freedom to mingle and her ability to maneuver the stairs that led treacherously toward the reception hall on the lower level. She was smiling and chatting but distracted as she grabbed onto the railing and tried to keep her balance one steep and slick step at a time. But oh no, her ankle twisted, she tripped and then watched helplessly as the car seat, still carrying Isabelle, escaped from her hand and slid solo down the staircase—landing safely, thank goodness, and upright at the bottom. Her newborn was unharmed, but poor Paige was badly shaken, her confidence swiftly drained by a frighteningly close call.

Things tend to go downhill once you start second-guessing yourself and when your hungry, tired baby reaches her limit. It was obvious now Paige would have to be leaving, although her husband and her sisters and her parents, all integral members of the wedding party, would stay and feast and dance and laugh and visit, unbound by a nursing, totally dependent, mom-craving daughter. "Goodbye!" said everyone, not without kindness, yet clearly detached from the loneliness and disappointment that darkened this joyous occasion for one inexperienced mother coming to terms with the all-consuming role she had entered into.

I'll bet each of us has a memory that comes immediately to mind, a specific recollection of a time or an event that drove home with painful clarity how isolating motherhood can be. For me it was a luncheon in downtown Chicago with several of our closest (childless) friends. Elijah was a toddler, maybe eighteen months old; it was naptime, but I pushed it anyway because, quite frankly, I was desperate for a reason to socialize.

From the get-go, my son was not interested in the high chair, nor amused by the small bag of toys I had packed to keep him entertained and charmingly quiet throughout a long, drawn-out meal in a fine restaurant. I was physically present but mentally and emotionally absent, offering up snacks and crayons and pleading with my little boy for cooperation. By the time we ordered wine, salad, and pasta, he was squirmier than I could handle inconspicuously. With tears on the brink of overflowing, and blowing my "in control" cover, I hastily repacked the diaper bag, swooped up my melting-down son, and apologized for having to take off so early. It was then, while crying in the street as I imagined the witty and articulate conversations taking place just as enjoyably without me, that I began (not without struggle, mind you) to own the seclusion.

What's harder, I sometimes wonder: trying to keep both our children and ourselves engaged and at peace within the walls of our Orthodox churches, where everywhere we turn we find a visual or auditory reminder of God's Kingdom; or being isolated in our homes, away from a community of other Orthodox Christians—or for that matter from anyone who can communicate without pointing and screeching?

It's a hefty responsibility we carry on our shoulders as parents, bringing Christ into the mundane—an environment in which we are constantly sidetracked from eternity by present credit card debts, grocery lists, chores, deadlines, and televised entertainment. There is so much I want to teach my children: manners, kindness, a love for reading, conscientiousness, how to manage a home, good stewardship, and of course the practices and theology of the Orthodox Church.

There are periods of time when I see these goals as exciting, when I feel competent to guide these little sponges soaking up my experience and wisdom toward a higher quality of life. But there are just as many, if not more, occasions when I feel that all I am capable of accomplishing is keeping them alive and in one piece until bedtime, when I'll collapse and wonder how I will make it through another day. All the same objectives that I previously viewed as rewarding will become taxing and impossible and demanding. I will curse my need for sleep and feel ashamed about wearing thin before the tasks I'd envisioned myself accomplishing have been attended to. My thoughts will rise up against me, and I will crumble.

You see, it's not just outside distractions or the absence of adult interaction that test a mother's resilience, but also her sense of urgency when it comes to making decisions about her children. Although other relatives, teachers, and godparents most certainly have a vested interest in their development, it is mom who oversees the daily schedules of her kids, who disciplines and dresses and feeds them. Every sniffle, temper tantrum, or insecurity points back, at least in her mind, to her strengths or weaknesses as a parent. As my good friend Elise put it, "When my son seems lonely, I agonize over his social life. His shyness becomes like a dangerous fire that only I am responsible for putting out."

We mothers tend to overthink and overanalyze, examining our kids through a magnifying glass and making mountains out of usually harmless molehills. Our combined love and solitude make us particularly susceptible to feelings of frustration and self-doubt. I was thinking about this recently, from an Orthodox perspective: how mothers and monastics, both crucial components of Christ's Church, tend to fight their spiritual battles within their minds. Due to our attachment to an interior type of living, where there is often little contact with the bigger world outside, there is less of a chance we'll be lured by lust, hatred, or greed to commit crimes against humanity worthy of newspaper headlines or watercooler tongue-wagging. I, for one, stay heedful of temptations to engage in flagrant sinfulness; but what I'm too soft and lax in protecting is my active thought life, and it is here that I am most often and brutally assaulted.

My friend Elise was talking with Paige and me about her struggles with depression and how for years she has been held captive by disparaging contemplations. She is a convert to Orthodoxy, and her love for the Church is so inspiring to me because I've witnessed firsthand the practical differences the Orthodox Church has made in her life for the better. On this specific occasion, we were discussing the topic of *logismoi,* a spiritual concept we had both recently read about in Kyriacos Markides' book, *The Mountain of Silence.*

Logismoi are essentially distracting thoughts that direct our attention away from Christ. I was intrigued by Elise's evaluation of the subject because I myself had found the notion of our minds being continually attacked by Satan so profound that it had totally revolutionized the way I dealt with envy, resentment, and anxiety. Our conversation only confirmed to me how great a potential a thorough understanding of logismoi and their harmful effects on our spirit has for healing a mother's weary soul. According to Father Maximos, a monk from Mount Athos and Markides' spiritual guide, there are five stages to an attack by logismoi:

1. **Assault:** *This stage occurs when we are first hit hard, from seemingly out of nowhere, with a spiteful, resentful, destructive, or terrifying idea. "When such a logismos strikes, no matter how sinful it may be, it does not render us accountable,"* Father Maximos explains. *"In simple language, we commit no sin. The holy elders throughout the ages were relentlessly tempted and assaulted by similar and even worse logismoi."*

2. **Interaction:** *When we begin to further explore our destructive thoughts ("Am I a horrible mother? What would happen if I did leave? How could I go on living if something*

were to happen to them?"), we raise the danger level a bit. But according to Father Maximos, we are still, at this juncture, not committing a sin. "The person can indeed examine such a logismos and consider several options without being accountable. But if the person is weak by temperament, then defeat may be the most likely outcome of that exposure to the logismos."

3. **Consent:** *By this point in the process, a decision has been reached and we are well on our way to giving in to the temptation that first struck us unawares, then captivated our imagination, and now has prompted us to proceed in a sinful manner.*

4. **Captivity:** *During this stage we act. We actually say and do something we shouldn't as a result of heeding the negative logismoi sent by Satan to obstruct our view of the Kingdom of heaven.*

5. **Passion:** *When we lose control and the wherewithal to fight back against the logismoi, becoming addicted to the damaging thoughts and behavior, we have succumbed to a passion. "The holy elders have warned us," said Father Maximos, "that when we become dominated by such passions it is like giving the key of our heart to Satan so that he can get in and out any time he wishes."* (The Mountain of Silence, Doubleday, pp. 124–130)

When they are all laid out this way, in such a clear and trackable manner, I can see so plainly how my own habitual progression through these stages could be halted if I simply paid attention and stayed alert. If I reacted less, and anticipated more the temptations designed to divert me from my full potential for peacefulness and freedom in Christ, I'd find depth and purpose in hardships I might otherwise interpret as shallow, pointless, and a huge waste of my time.

Such decisive introspection, as endorsed by the Church and her Fathers, does not come naturally to those accustomed to the breakneck speed at which our society prefers to travel—perhaps in a vain attempt to distance ourselves from mortality and the disturbing possibilities regarding our enslavement to it that snake their way into our psyche when the mind slows down.

In an article entitled "Waiting and Watching," Fr. John Breck reflects on the imperative necessity of our "maintaining an inner attentiveness or vigilance" as Orthodox Christians called to follow in the footsteps of our most holy ancestors: the saints, martyrs, and monastics who learned through fasting and continuous prayer to shut out superfluous input and hone in on rewards eternal. He writes:

> For most of us, whether we are conscious of it or not, life consists essentially in "waiting." The hyper-activism that characterizes American life, and the life of most Western societies today, distracts us enough from what is essential, that we have lost touch with the real meaning and value of being alive. We are "waiting for Godot" rather than for "the one thing needful." To acquire that "one thing," however, we need to shift our focus, reacquire a sense of genuine value (and civility), reorganize our priorities, and reject the artificial virtues society inculcates in us: aggressive competition, perfectionism, status, and material gain. We need to discover once again the truth that the wealthiest among us is the monk who has renounced every possession and obtained the "glorious liberty of the children of God." We need to find peace and happiness not in the marketplace or in accumulating "stuff," but in assuming the inner struggle of attentiveness, of watchfulness, which alone leads to "every blessing of the age to come." (http://www.oca.org)

We should all set our sights high, of course, keeping the obtaining of that eventual "glorious liberty" our primary aim as Orthodox Christians. But how, on a practical level (for those of us who are still very much novices), do we even begin to arrive at a place where we can not only recognize the logismoi for what they are but also nip their harmful effects in the bud?

What's the first thing we should do when we are blind-sided by disturbing suggestions? Erik Bohlin, an Orthodox Christian counselor and host of the website, orthodoxcoun-selor.com, suggests (are you ready for this?) nothing!

> *We ignore them. That is what the Church fathers tell us to do. They explain that they are like flies and we are to bat them away. From a neurological perspective this makes perfect sense. We don't want to think about the thought or even dialogue with it as it will grow even more. The brain cells that we neglect will eventually die. This should give any of us hope who has struggled with unwanted thoughts. When the logismoi, like the unwanted salesman comes to the door, we are to shut the door and not to even dialogue with him. To invite him into our house or our heart constitutes sin—sin of the heart. (http://orthodoxcounselor.com/logismoi.htm)*

I cannot tell you how many nights I have lain awake trying to reason myself out of anxiousness or dread or low self-esteem:

"You're not organized or patient enough."

"You are totally inept as a mother."

"That raspy cough of Mary's is only going to worsen and make her gravely ill."

"You will never have a clean house or time to yourself again."

When these negative views of what I knew deep down was a very blessed life reared their ugly and shameful heads, my former habit was to dissect and reflect obsessively on their possible origins. The more I tried to talk myself out of being scared or angry or depressed, the tighter a rein did the logismoi seem to have on me. Surely I was a weak Christian, useless and ineffective, if I was harboring so much doubtfulness.

What I wasn't grasping, however, and what had never been explained to me previously, was that all that destructive input was being fired upon my spirit like poisoned arrows rather than coming from within. It wasn't sinful to be suddenly ambushed by a harsh or even cruel contemplation on marriage or motherhood. I wasn't in the wrong for thinking unkind things about my neighbor—if, that is, I refused to feed those impulses with gossip, discrimination, or further speculations and assumptions. With that awareness came the freedom to move forward.

Sometimes I could swear I will start screaming if I hear the phrase, "Mom! Priscilla (or Ben, or Mary, or Elijah) won't share (or stop, or listen, or do every single thing I ask her to)!" just one more time. It used to be that my annoyance could start an avalanche of regrettable behavior both on my part and that of my children. I handled parenting like a diet; I would make a change and stick with it—no cheating, no compromising, no allowances for weakness. If, heaven forbid, I did succumb to temptation, such as a forbidden bowl of ice cream or a harsh word spoken, I considered myself a failure and thus surrendered my willpower entirely, resisting nothing.

How much saner it is not to dwell on our mistakes or to

feed their ravenous hunger for our attention. Yes, I screwed up—Lord, have mercy! Now get over it! Let us redeem the moment in front of us by apologizing and returning our focus to Christ.

Over the last ten years, I have read every type of childrearing book, article, blog, or interview in existence, and while I can usually identify partly with what their authors are revealing about their own mothering experiences, I tend to feel isolated even further from mainstream society by my Orthodox viewpoints on birth, education, fulfillment, and sacrifice. For example, I know of few other women in my neighborhood with young children at home who are fasting half the year, trying to explain the difference between Pascha and Western Easter (especially if they are weeks apart!), or who are racking their brains for ways to make namedays truly special.

I am deeply entrenched in my faith; every decision I make as a mom is born out of an Orthodox mindset. Because of this, I do not hold to the commonly held assumptions that easier is better, retaining my own identity is paramount, or prayers are considered answered only when a burden is lifted. I certainly don't find motherhood to be one hundred percent enjoyable or its inherent dilemmas solvable by way of clever tricks and perfect discipline techniques. I do believe, however, that motherhood is spiritually rewarding and salvific.

Orthodoxy is unique in its ability to bring women out of their emotional ruts and into the satisfaction of growth and stability by way of the Eucharist, confession, and theology. The Church provides a myriad of tangible opportunities for disentangling ourselves from deception, delusion, and despair. The more actively we participate in the life of the Orthodox Church, taking our cues on how to proceed during times of both joy and sadness from the writings of our Church Fathers, the mystical illumination found within the sacraments, and the Scriptures, the more meaningful will become the strenuous task of learning patience and self-control through prayerful mothering.

While working on this chapter, I had a conversation with Elijah. Something was weighing on his heart, but he was hesitant to share it with me; so he began to talk around the real issue at hand.

"Do you ever have thoughts, Mom, that aren't so good?"

"All the time," I assured him. "How about you?"

"Uh huh." He looked down to avoid making eye contact. "Sometimes I get tempted to do things I probably shouldn't." And so I sat with him and shared a little of what I'd learned about thoughts and temptations—about logismoi. This was a rare and fantastic opportunity to bring a concept so powerful and spiritually significant into the realm of his own preadolescent experiences. I prayed for mercy and proceeded with caution, lest I either minimize the magnitude of these early wrestlings with sin or come off as too grave and unapproachable.

"You know, sweetheart, it isn't wrong to suddenly have feelings that seem mean or dishonest. Those feelings are being shot at you like bullets as a way to keep you from remembering God's goodness, forgiveness, and love. There is even a complicated-sounding name for them: logismoi. The logismoi begin weakening us with those thoughts that aren't so good, and then slowly take over our willpower, if we let them. But fortunately, there's a way to gain control when we're overwhelmed."

"How would you handle . . . sneaking?" he asked, slowly and cautiously gauging my facial expression as he proceeded. When I didn't display anger, he went on with, "It's just that I've been sneaking a lot lately. Things like cookies or time on my Gameboy, and I feel pretty bad about it, but it's hard to stop."

"Well, that's a perfect example!" I said. "I'll explain to you about logismoi within that specific context. First, you might think, 'Mom said only one cookie, but I'd rather have three.'" At this he nodded knowingly, and I made a mental note to myself to find a different hiding spot for our after-dinner treats.

"Next, you might explore that idea in more detail. 'Who would ever know if I took another one?' you'd possibly ask yourself. 'I'd probably never get caught.' Then you're well on your way to stage three of the logismos, when you would actually devise a plan for getting hold of some extra cookies without me noticing. Stage four takes place when you go ahead and commit the sin by pulling a chair up to our pantry, taking the cookies out of the box, and sticking them in your mouth before I can catch you. Stage five would be kind of like an addiction. When the urge to sneak came upon you, you'd be powerless to prevent it from taking root in your soul. The logismos would rule over you like a tyrant ruling a slave."

Surprisingly (or maybe I shouldn't have been surprised at all), this all made perfect sense to my son. It felt amazing to be able to share with him a most potent defense against the wiles of the devil in the form of awareness and the Jesus Prayer. "All you have to do," I said, "is call out to God with, 'Lord Jesus Christ, have mercy on me!' and He will hear you and give you the strength to disregard the lies and deceitful suggestions being hurled in your direction."

We prayed right then and there, and I was inspired as never before to be vigilant in my filtering out of unhealthful stimuli. Life is challenging enough already without the added pressure of expecting ourselves, on our own, to gain victory in a vicious battle for our sanity and well-being. In this case, less is more. Our best tactic here is to simplify by letting go and allowing Christ to win it for us.

Although it may feel much of the time as if no one else quite understands the intensity of being "on" twenty-four hours a day, or the roller coaster of emotions we mothers ride daily, let us take comfort and courage in our shared pursuit of righteousness and in the utter invincibility of our resurrected Savior. I may never have the privilege of meeting you in person, but even from a distance we are bonded. Through our faithfulness we have the capacity to uplift one another, for each time we resist the empty persuasions of hell, it benefits the body of Christ as a whole. Let us pray for the wisdom to cease trying by our own strength, and start crawling out of our same old tired ruts by surrendering our weak and fragile wills into the hands of God.

Chapter Ten

Education

*L*ast spring our small town was hit with a slew of storms. One in particular was especially violent. The wind outside was raging. Our windows quivered with each reverberation of thunder that swelled in the muggy air and finally exploded like a hand grenade.

I expected my children would be terrified, so I waited for the screams, straining my neck toward the staircase, listening for my cue to hold a hand, wipe a tear, or whisper into tiny ears that everything would be all right. But the deep sleep afforded to the young had already worked its magic; I could hear nothing in terms of fear from the second story of our old Victorian as it swayed in time with the riotous weather. "Hmm," I thought, "they might not need me after all."

I read a book, washed a few dishes, and got the coffeepot ready for its morning brew before finally calling it quits and heading to my room.

"Mom?" I barely heard as I passed the metal bunk beds on my way to the cool cotton sheets and memory foam pillow beckoning me to bid this day adieu.

"Elijah?" I whispered back. "What in the world are you

doing? It's past ten o'clock, you'll be exhausted tomorrow if you don't get some rest."

"Mom," he repeated just as quietly, "I'm having a hard time settling down."

"The storm?" I asked, and he nodded with a bit of sheepishness in his eyes. "I'm sorry to be a bother," he added.

"Scoot over," I whispered as I climbed up the ladder, careful not to wake his four-year-old brother. Since no one could see us lying in the dark, Elijah snuggled into me without embarrassment.

"It's really creepy in here at night with all the creaky noises. Sometimes I can hardly stand it. Do you think we're going to have a tornado? Do you think robbers could come down through the attic?"

"No, honey, I really don't, but I do understand what it's like to be scared. At night our mind plays tricks on us. The things we see, hear, and think about all day long without concern get bigger, uglier, and spookier when the lights go out and everything is quiet. Even moms get fooled every once in awhile." Like most evenings, lately, but that part I kept to myself. I have always been a worrier, a trait that has become more cumbersome as my age, responsibilities, and blessings have increased—loud, cuddly, demanding blessings embedded within my heart like crown jewels. I have spent countless dark hours fighting my anxieties, longing for the hopefulness of morning.

"As Christians," I told my Elijah—I told myself, "we shouldn't lead lives that are crippled by fear. There is, unfortunately, a lot of evil to obsess over in this world, but we must keep our focus on Christ's Resurrection. Jesus conquered death, and we need not let it paralyze us any longer."

Together, we sang, "Holy God, Holy Mighty, Holy Immortal have mercy on us," until our eyelids began to droop and Elijah's rigid body melted in the warmth of our shared supplications. I kissed him on the forehead, full of thankfulness for a moment of spiritual refreshment I hadn't even known I was thirsty for.

"How generous," I thought while tiptoeing out into the hallway, "to bless me through the comforting of my son."

Jesus said, "Assuredly, I say to you, whoever does not receive the kingdom of God as a little child will by no means enter it" (Mark 10:15). This is a tall order for adults too tired, realistic, and disappointed to foster within themselves the natural unselfconsciousness that makes kids such wholehearted believers. And yet, while going back in time would be impossible and, let's face it, quite exhausting, we can reclaim some of the freshness of our youth through the eyes of our sons, daughters, nieces, nephews, and godchildren, as they savor the moments we learned slowly over time to ignore. Children can be a powerful inspiration, capable of renewing and replenishing our faith, if we pause within our busyness to participate in their interior development. Through our instinct to guide, through the openness of tender minds, and through the questions we are called upon to answer, God reveals Himself. Through the shedding of our selfishness, through love unconditional, and through increased prayers for wisdom and patience, a spark of devotion for Christ and His Church can be fanned into flames hot and raging.

About a year into motherhood, it finally sank in that the disruptions in church were not going to be a temporary problem, easily solved by way of good solid discipline. My toddler had a mind of his own, a will of his own, and a soul of his own to be handled with care and consistency. An understanding of and appreciation for a service that cut into playtime and severely restricted his freedom to wiggle and use the much-preferred "outside voice" would not be automatic. Instilling a love for the liturgy would take years of work and intentional direction.

For a long time I worried that all the effort I was putting forth to keep loud whispers quiet, busy legs still, and a restless mind occupied would hinder my growth as an Orthodox Christian. I mourned the loss of my initial church experience—more reverent and less eventful.

I remember one frustrating Pascha spent down in the basement nursing, rocking, and quieting screams of over-tiredness. After weeks of Lent, I was missing it—the joy, the brightness, and all the songs of triumph. I pouted, I sulked, I felt sorry for myself until in passing I heard a fellow parishioner talking about his wife, who was ill and had stayed home that evening, just as disappointed as I was. "Well," he said with conviction, "Christ is still risen! She can certainly rejoice in that!"

To me, that was a revolutionary insight. My physical participation, or lack thereof, in the prayers and shouts of "Christos Voskrese!" did not change the fact, the miracle, of Christ being raised from the dead. That one alteration to my way of thinking helped pave the way for a whole new understanding of worship.

There are natural seasons in life. There are moments we are called to soak in the love of God and moments we are asked to share that love with others. In the beginning stages of my conversion, my act of obedience was simply to learn. But now as a mother I was also to teach, and through teaching begin to apply the commandments of Christ, centered on self-denial. There is a very real difference between biding our time until children get old enough to control themselves in public and using our time to guide them toward salvation.

Before I had kids, my other commitments made it difficult to view establishing our own traditions for fasts, feasts, and namedays as a priority. But when suddenly I was trusted with the responsibility of raising a family, I found the motivation necessary to search books, pick brains, and gather supplies that would help to create a home-based rhythm of faith parallel with that of the Church. Our evening prayers became more regular as Troy and I sought out ways to make Christ a significant part of the everyday lives of our four young children. My instructions and explanations, generously poured out on Saturday evenings and Sunday mornings, to stand, to bow, to cross oneself with three fingers pinched together signifying the Holy Trinity, were not mere interruptions to my own quest for spiritual fulfillment but rather a sacrifice, an offering of my first fruits to God.

With supervision comes accountability, with accountability comes the call to serve, and through service to those within our care comes freedom from selfishness and time-wasting pursuits—pursuits that could never even begin to improve our quality of life as can instilling a legacy of belief to be passed like a treasured inheritance from one generation to the next.

My third child, Benjamin, was just three years old when I explained to him how to prepare for the coming of St. Nicholas. "Go get your shoe," I said, "and bring it to Mommy, and then we'll put a carrot inside for his donkey."

"Okay!" he responded without the slightest bit of confusion, without question, without hesitancy. If I'd asked him to fill that shoe with Jell-o and stick it in the mailbox, I am certain I would have gotten the exact same enthusiastic response. That night, when the kids were tucked in bed, I delighted in the little sneakers and Mary Janes lining our front door, awaiting the arrival of the kindly saint, who would exchange the vegetables for chocolate coins and a small present to tuck into each of them. I sifted flour onto the floor and had Troy come and step on it, making footprints in the "snow" that would prove St. Nicholas had been present in our home.

I was honestly just as excited as our children, tossing and turning and waiting for the sun to rise, signaling that St. Nicholas Day had begun. "Wake up!" I yelled. "Wake up! Someone special has been by for a visit." Their puffy eyes took a moment to adjust, but then BAM! they were off with squeals of excitement to see for themselves what treats St. Nicholas had left behind. That afternoon, as together we read stories about his life—our favorite being his secret plan to meet the financial needs of three sisters by dropping coins in their stockings hung up to dry—I had no qualms in saying, "Yes! St. Nicholas is real!" Inspired by my own kids' flagrant acceptance of that which cannot be defined using reason, I took pleasure in having the freedom to embrace the mystery of a saint who fell asleep in the Lord centuries ago but who readily intercedes on our behalf.

It is hard to pinpoint the exact age when I began to view all things supernatural with automatic suspicion and doubt. I could accept (because it is generally accepted by the masses) that babies grow in bellies, that caterpillars transform into butterflies, and that spring appears at the end of every winter. But a weeping icon? the presence of Christ in the Eucharist? accounts of monks who were visited by their patron saints? These were more difficult to swallow.

The more knowledge I gained about the laws of probability, the less likely I became to take such miracles at face value. Blithely, I would pick and choose what to interpret as "literal" and what to define as "figurative," based upon what . . . I don't know. But somewhere in the retelling of these biblical stories and traditional accounts to my children, whose eyes grew wide at the mention of Jonah's sojourn in a whale's stomach, Mary being accepted into heaven body and soul after her death, or "the great cloud of witnesses" present with us every Sunday, I retired my spiritual inhibitions and gave birth to a fresh sense of awe and wonder at the power and glory of the gospel message.

"But God has chosen the foolish things of the world to put to shame the wise," says Paul in 1 Corinthians 1:27, "and God has chosen the weak things of the world to put to shame the things which are mighty." Nobody likes to appear stupid, naïve, or gullible, but that is exactly the risk we take once we pick up our cross and follow Jesus.

I have caught myself in the past trying to spin my beliefs in such a way that I came across as an intellectual kind of Christian. I wanted to make God and myself appear relevant and enlightened. But my children, once they heard about Jesus and His birth and His death and Resurrection, not knowing the stigma behind an outright defiance of science and common sense, began boldly proclaiming their convictions without squeamishness. And this is what the Lord has asked us to emulate, a childlike love so pure that neither naysayers nor public opinion can dampen it, a humility so genuine we think nothing of ourselves, either positive or negative, for we ourselves have been emptied to make room for the Savior of this world.

"*Is God* really in this Church with us?"
"Does my guardian angel really watch me while I sleep?"
"If the devil apologized, would God take him back?"
"How can Jesus and God and the Holy Spirit all be one?"

These are just a taste of the questions I have fielded over the years, some much easier to answer than others. The older my children get, the more complicated the inquiries become. Sometimes I feel frustrated that I don't have more to offer, that my words seem to tangle up and oppose each other. I want to have the perfect response, a response guaranteed to carry them into adulthood without skepticism or turning away from Orthodoxy. I try not to let my emotions, my desperation for the salvation of their souls, take over and send me into a panic. Surely their curiosity indicates fascination; I should be more concerned if they were indifferent, uninterested in the depths and details of a borrowed conviction. It is essential, during times like this, that I ask forgiveness for my doubtfulness, that I remember my place as an educator, not a hypnotist. My job is to guide and to pray; the rest is in the hands of God.

I have been blessed over the last ten years with knowledgeable spiritual fathers, priests from whom I have received Holy Communion and with whom I have participated in the Sacrament of Confession. Their explanations of certain tenets of Orthodoxy have been very helpful, but what has most inspired me to "press toward the goal for the prize of the upward call of God in Christ Jesus" (Philippians 3:14) are their personal examples of steadfastness within their parishes, their families, and their faith.

Now is the time to show my kids what Christianity is really about, and to supplement that living illustration with whatever spiritual clarification the Holy Spirit provides, through lips dependent on His wisdom. Their natural curiosity is a huge incentive to me to shun the hypocrisy of saying one thing and doing another, of sending mixed messages about authenticity. When little eyes are watching, I am reminded that God is also watching, that life is not lived in a vacuum.

There is purpose in every seemingly trivial undertaking from folding laundry, to wiping spills, to the humming of hymns in a darkened bedroom curled up with an anxious son. There are, mercifully, bountiful opportunities in every new day, hour, and minute to break bad habits and to stretch ourselves a little bit further for the sake of the cross, the Church, and our children.

"Have great care of your children. We live at a time when much freedom is given to the expression of thought, but little care is taken that thoughts should be founded on truth. Teach them to love truth," said the Elder Macarius of Optina. These are unprecedented times in our society. More than ever before do our kids have access, through television, internet, peers, and aggressive advertising, to seductive distractions intent on luring them away from the reality that money, fame, and power bring only emptiness and an insatiable longing for that which can never truly satisfy. If we are not proactive in countering those lies with a Christ-centered Orthodox perspective, there is a much greater chance we will lose our children to the titillating influences of secularism.

There was a time when I was very intimidated by the prospect of explaining the ins and outs of Orthodoxy to my children. What I knew like the back of my hand was the Protestant faith I'd been taught and retaught in Sunday school classes via flannel graph stories, crafts, and catchy songs. I was devoted to the Orthodox Church but unversed in her language and "big T" and "little t" traditions: Ambo? Prokeimenon? No kneeling between Pascha and Pentecost? Holy water? You might as well stick me in a Barnes & Noble and tell me to sum up for each of my children the contents of all the books on all the shelves.

In Orthodoxy, everything means something. How in the world was I supposed to familiarize myself with such an abundance of terminology, symbolism, and important dates in time to have it all make sense for my kids before they became teenagers? Where would one even begin in terms of order? Should I focus on the twelve major feasts or the meaning of icons? How about the specifics of each service, including Divine Liturgy, Vespers, and Matins?

It was similar to the apprehension I had felt about teaching my six-year-old son to read while I was homeschooling him in Chicago. What about the soft and hard "G" sounds? How would he know "P" and "H" together sound like "F"? How would he make sense of a silent "E"? But then miraculously, the more we read together, just enjoying the stories themselves while I casually but consistently pointed out the various nuances of language, he began to make use of context, decoding mysterious symbols and seeing past the sounds to seize their meaning.

Orthodoxy is best taught through immersion. That was definitely true for me, and I am trusting my children will learn likewise. Peering into it from the outside, I'd felt hopeless about mastering all the "rules" and specifics of this ancient faith, still new to me and quite dauntingly unfamiliar. But then I was chrismated, trusting only that my respect for the Church would eventually spawn wisdom. And wouldn't you know it, the more I participated over the years that followed in the sacraments and services of my home parish, the more I gradually internalized what had once seemed so difficult to grasp.

This dropping of the scales from my eyes was and continues to be a very slow process. Sometimes there are "aha!" moments, such as during a homily or in the midst of a book chapter, when something will suddenly strike a chord with me and I'll be changed by the newly acquired knowledge. Just as many times, however, the revelations seem to come from out of nowhere. A barrier I'd thought impossible to get over, such as the veneration of Mary or a relationship with my patron saint, will inexplicably crumble, allowing me to unabashedly embrace a doctrine I had wanted to comprehend but couldn't.

Such breakthroughs remind me that an understanding of divine blessings is under God's dominion; my responsibility lies solely in showing up and enduring patiently the bouts of doubt, silence, and confusion. Where does one begin? With a prayer of "Lord, have mercy," and a pliable spirit willing to forsake intellect for the sake of mystery. This acceptance of what cannot be defined or summed up using facts or logic is what I hope to instill first within my children, like a solid foundation of awe and expectation on which to build a lifetime of learning about Christ and His one holy and apostolic Church.

I am pleased to say there are a growing number of resources now available for teaching parents and children both about the Orthodox Faith. I use the ones I've discovered thus far as references for defining terminology, clarifying concepts, and generating ideas to make namedays and feast days more special. *Let us Attend,* a podcast on Ancient Faith Radio, for example, offers a simplified version of each Sunday's Gospel reading as well as accompanying thought questions that my kids can meditate on before Divine Liturgy; having that familiarity with the passage being read by our priest, they tend to listen more attentively during the actual service.

For remembering special traditions, such as what to include in a Pascha basket, when to bring fruit to church (August 6—the Feast of the Transfiguration, in case you were wondering), when to have and what to do at a house blessing, and so forth, I refer to my *Building an Orthodox Christian Family* handbook, published by the Orthodox Christian Schools of Northeast Ohio. Each year I incorporate a few more of the many craft and activity ideas as my children mature and start to lengthen their notoriously short attention spans. Just recently, Orthodox-mom blogs have been sprouting up all over the Internet, providing a sense of community and camaraderie that is all too often missing in the "un-Orthodox" neighborhoods many of us abide in. These women are sharing tips, personal experiences, and links to other like-minded mothers who are also writing about their Orthodox lives and families.

When I am able to view all this accessible information as, let's say, the style-enhancing details of a carefully designed living space rather than as a checklist of mandatory building materials without which our house would surely crumble, I enjoy figuring out ways to apply Orthodoxy to the everyday experiences of my unique family members. What happens all too often, however, is that instead of praying for wisdom and opportunities to share the beauty of our Faith with my children, I cease depending on Christ for guidance and declare myself their sole educator. I stack heavily on my own shoulders unattainable ambitions, such as fully digesting all the advice and doctrinal specifics I've come across over the years in order to regurgitate, verbatim, every last bit of it to my dependents. There is a fine line between nourishing and force-feeding, which I am trusting the Holy Spirit will help me balance—that is, if I am diligent about asking Him to. The goal here is not to make sure my children have all the right answers, but to convey an applicable and holistic comprehension of the Church and her sacraments.

This can, at times, be a wearisome undertaking, especially when our children seem indifferent to the spiritual principles we want so badly to instill within them. A glazed-over stare during family scripture readings, squirminess and silliness throughout evening prayers, or an exasperated sigh at having to go to church again can be discouraging to a parent who wants only to pass down to the next generation her own devotion to Christ. I've caught myself more than once being overly stern with such childish reactions, simply because I was hurt or disappointed by what I imagined was a purposeful display of disrespect for both myself and the values I hold most dear. It is imperative in those instances that I distance myself emotionally for a moment and remember that at this point I am mostly preparing the soil and planting seeds to bloom later—maybe tomorrow, maybe in a month, maybe a decade from now when the rigors of adult life prove too strenuous to handle solo and the abstract truths often explained to them in childhood become a balm to soothe the soreness of their humanity.

When Elijah was six years old, I would read to him daily from our assigned homeschooling chapter books. We'd start off side by side on our couch for oh, maybe three minutes or so before his body would start to twitch from the discomfort of being contained. First his knee would begin to bounce, then his head would start to wobble, back and forth like a bobble-head doll. "Be still," I'd demand of him, "and listen!"

"I am listening!" he'd whine. "Can I please sit somewhere else?" Most mornings I'd relent out of tiredness, with firm directions that he lie quietly on the floor or curl up attentively in the rocking chair. This he would do for another few minutes before kicking his legs, lifting his shirt over his head, or arching his back and making clucking noises with his tongue.

"That's enough!" I'd shout, clearly annoyed by his restlessness. "Go wait on your bed until you're ready to pay attention." Then he would cry, and I would fume because another morning had been wasted by his refusal to cooperate.

One day, however, after an identical altercation, I decided to call his bluff and make him summarize for me the book passage he had just wiggled through. To my great surprise, he had absolutely no problem doing so. In fact, he did like the story we were reading; he wasn't trying to be naughty or defiant.

I learned, my usual hard way, that just because my children aren't staring eagerly into my eyes or hanging breathlessly on every wise word coming out of my mouth, that does not mean they haven't processed what I've just told them. Every once in awhile, I'm even rewarded with irrefutable evidence that my hard work has not been in vain. I was delighted when, after listening absentmindedly to many recitations of accounts from the life of St. Nicholas, my kids were able to provide detailed descriptions of his miraculous acts of mercy to a visiting friend.

As my children get older, I am encouraged by the conversations that have been presenting themselves with greater frequency while preparing for feasts, confession, or Eucharist. As much as I sometimes wish I could bypass their fiery wills and encode within their souls a longing for salvation, having to swallow that urge to control them and instead focus more intently on filling our home with visual and verbal reminders of God's Kingdom actually strengthens my relationship with Christ and with the kids. Just as I am never abandoned despite the seasons of both passionate reverence and lukewarm apathy, I can best serve my family by loving them unconditionally throughout their spiritual ups and downs, adding validity to our faith by consistently serving Christ by serving others.

I want their Orthodox education to be a seamless component of their overall existence, not segmented into a category of its own. Our familial practices, including prostrating before one another and asking for forgiveness in preparation for the Eucharist; singing the appropriate troparion for a specific feast day before meals; and reading stories from the lives of saints before bedtime, act as twine binding each of us to one another and to the life of the Church. I pray that the connection between what we teach them and the way we live will be inseparable. Education is, in this context, as education does. How I apply the material I teach speaks volumes about its worth and authenticity. More important than what I know is what I am willing to surrender—for their sake, for your sake, and ultimately for the sake of our salvation.

Chapter Eleven

Permeation

*W*hen my older brother, Bobby, was fifteen years old, he wore a retainer. Upon receiving it, he got lectures from my parents about crooked teeth and the value of a dollar which he heeded for the most part, except on one occasion: That day, the rather expensive little appliance that should have been put back safely in his mouth was discarded along with his lunch bag and forgotten. When my mother picked us up from school that afternoon, she questioned him about it and then, oh no, he remembered. So they walked back to the cafeteria and were told that the trash had already been emptied. My mother replied, "Where?" and they were led to the large gray dumpster in the school parking lot.

"Well," Mom said to Bobby matter-of-factly, "let's get started."

My brother's face then contorted into an expression of horror as he suddenly understood her ingenious plan. "I have to get in there!?" he whined, pointing to the sour-smelling pile of refuse containing sights and textures he didn't want to look at, much less wade through.

"It was pretty gross," Mom remembers, when asked to tell me the story again from her perspective, "but there was no way we were going to pay for a brand new retainer when I knew that a perfectly good one was hiding somewhere within all that garbage." Fully understanding he had no leverage with which to bargain, Bobby took a deep breath and joined our mother in foraging through food scraps and brown paper bags for a napkin containing the dental apparatus they hoped would be discovered sooner, much sooner, rather than later.

Figuring this was Bobby's lesson to learn, I'd lain low up until this point on a nearby bench pretending to do my homework. I was happily forgotten about until my brother opened a sack inside which was my entire lunch (packed lovingly that morning by my considerate mother), completely uneaten—most likely because I'd scrounged up enough change to buy soda and some French fries instead. It was my turn, then, to feel the frustration of an overworked and underappreciated parent standing knee deep in filth and gazing disappointedly on her irresponsible son and wasteful daughter.

Eventually, believe it or not, they would find that lost retainer and Bobby would manage to hang onto it for another seven years. I, meanwhile, would be schooled on the concept of a budget and how purchasing items at a grocery store only to throw them away unconsumed is generally considered poor stewardship. For kids growing up in a culture infamous around the globe for its flippancy and excess, developing a sense of gratitude for the necessities that nourish and sustain us can be difficult.

Twenty years later, I am contemplating my mother's plight. Our children are at that age where when they ask you for a bomb pop from the ice cream truck and your response is, "I don't have money for that right now," they look at you suspiciously, because of course you have money—you're an adult! I can't blame them, really; it sure does appear as if everything is accessible, at least if you want it badly enough. Credit cards, adjustable rate mortgages, and divorce lawyers are great for plowing through all kinds of pesky barriers between the happiness we deserve and our state of discontent; nothing's out of reach in this day and age. This is why, perhaps, the Orthodox Faith, to many Americans, seems especially austere, and dare I say it, even somewhat superstitious, what with all those sacramental hoops one must jump through to get to God.

Throughout the early stages of my conversion, during conversations with friends who questioned the appropriateness of a theology that endorsed formal confession, fasting before Eucharist, overly scripted services, and a whole host of other hocus-pocusy looking practices such as chanting, incense burning, candle lighting, and icon kissing, I fumbled through attempted explanations of the balance between wanting to earn God's approval and presumptuously assuming that no efforts are required. I was still in analytical mode, trying to win over my well-intentioned skeptics with the perfect combination of scriptural and historical facts. But a deep-seated appreciation for the resurgence of holiness within our spiritually lackadaisical society is best acquired by way of firsthand experience. Until your own soul has transcended the innate limitations of time, casualness, and rationality, it is hard to comprehend how respect for Christ in the form of an adherence to ancient traditions and asceticism can actually intensify your appreciation of God's grace and goodness.

This past week, my son Benjamin unearthed a bright red egg from within the ominous recesses of our refrigerator.

"Cool, Mom," he said, "Look at this! Can I eat it?"

"That's probably not a good idea," I answered, before going on to explain how eggs are susceptible to spoilage if not consumed in a timely manner. The question we then had to ask ourselves was what to do with something that had been part of a basket full of treats, all blessed by our priest after the Paschal Divine Liturgy. I'll tell you, it was a privilege—an honor to pass on to my family our Orthodox conviction that there certainly remain in this world plenty of things to take very seriously.

"We believe," I told them, "as Orthodox Christians, that because this egg was set aside and sprinkled with holy water for the purpose of celebrating Jesus' Resurrection, it would be better to bury or burn it than to let it sit and mingle with old and stinky trash in a garbage dump." This made perfect sense to my children, whose hearts have not yet become tainted by more "mature" tendencies toward the embracing of cynicism—toward a lack of admiration for ceremonious displays of reverence.

The kids and I grabbed a shovel from the garage and loosened a patch of soil next to our strawberry plants. Priscilla carefully laid the egg in the space we had created for it; its brilliant shade of crimson contrasted dramatically with the subdued tones in the surrounding rocks and grass.

I'd been impatient that morning, more flustered than usual by the bickering, and accumulating chores hindering substantially my ability to rejoice in God's provision. Having to pause in the middle of my busyness in order to dispose reverently of a Paschal leftover, a symbol of our victory over death, was like a calming yet firm hand on my shoulder directing my attention away from the draining weariness of motherhood and onto the goal of salvation. Rather than detracting from Christ's redemptive work on the Cross, I promise you that the richness I see, smell, hear, taste, and touch within the Orthodox Church, throughout this journey toward the Kingdom of heaven, makes me all the more aware of my dependence on His compassion—makes me that much more grateful for these tangible and sacred opportunities to be reminded of His mercy.

What sets Orthodoxy apart, at least in my humble opinion, is its concreteness, its substance, and its texture. By nature, I am a wanderer; I simply do not have it in me to stay the course. Thanks to my family and evangelical background, I developed throughout my childhood a real and true love for Jesus Christ, but what I struggled with through adolescence and early adulthood was long-lasting growth. I seemed always to be grinding my wheels, trying harder and harder, yet never actually advancing in either distance or depth.

In my spiritual arsenal were worship songs, sermons, and "quiet times" (a period of time set aside in my day for spontaneous prayer and personal meditations on specific Bible passages). Each required my deliberate contemplation—a thorough application of my thoughts and emotions to the words being sung, read, or listened to. Such discipline produced knowledge of Christ's promises and expectations, but it required continuous mental and emotional participation. For a drifter like myself, whose mind has a tendency to wander and whose anxieties can easily sabotage all feelings of courage or empathy or love, my failure to stay spiritually engaged brought on devastating guilt and a dirty little habit of sometimes fudging my level of commitment by adopting the appropriate walk and talk of a Christian. What I didn't know I needed—or was even available—was a means to access God independent of my moods or preferences or fluctuating enthusiasm for the gospel message.

"Stand up," I whispered to Priscilla as our priest began the epiclesis portion of the Divine Liturgy, entreating the Holy

Spirit to mystically change the bread and wine into the Body and Blood of Christ. "Listen," I went on, "we are witnessing right now a true miracle."

"But Mom," she answered skeptically, like a kid second-guessing the legitimacy of the tooth fairy or flying reindeer, "isn't it really still just bread and normal wine?"

"No," I assured her in my most serious voice. "During Eucharist, we take Jesus into our bodies, and isn't that both mind-blowing and altogether comforting at the same time?"

I will also be explaining, as Priscilla and her siblings become older and more curious, that during confession, after we repent before God in the church, with a priest as our witness and spiritual counselor, our sins will be officially absolved, never again to smother us. My sins used to smother me, when I would privately ask for forgiveness before no one and then secretly continue to carry that burden on my shoulders—because I was pretty sure God heard me, but then again I hadn't felt forgiven, so who really knew?

"O Heavenly King," we will pray as a family hundreds of times over the next several years in the morning and before going to bed, "O Comforter, Spirit of Truth, who are everywhere present and fill all things, treasury of good things and Giver of life, come and abide in us and cleanse us from our sins, and save our souls, O Good One." At one time such repetition would have felt much too formulaic and spiritually stifling, but now when I teach to my own kids the ancient prayers of the Orthodox Church I will tell them how blessed we are to have access to these words, so tried and true and divinely inspired.

Last night, when all was finally quiet, I read this prayer by Metropolitan Philaret:

My Lord, I know not what I ought to ask of Thee.
Thou and Thou alone knowest my needs.
Thou lovest me more than I am able to love Thee.
O Father, grant unto me, Thy servant, all which I cannot ask.
For a cross I dare not ask, nor for consolation;
I dare only to stand in Thy presence.
My heart is open to Thee.
Thou seest my needs of which I myself am unaware.
Behold and lift me up!
In Thy presence I stand,
awed and silenced by Thy will and Thy judgments,
into which my mind cannot penetrate.
To Thee I offer myself as a sacrifice.
No other desire is mine but to fulfill Thy will.
Teach me how to pray.
Do Thyself pray within me.
Amen.

If you happened to skim these lines, I implore you to go back and read them thoroughly, because . . . WOW! Each sentiment they contain could be meditated on for a lifetime.

You see, truth be told, I usually haven't the foggiest idea of what is best, I mean really best, for my loved ones or myself. Left to my own devices, of course I would pray for extra speedy deliverance from every single one of our trials. And while there is absolutely nothing wrong with unscripted intercessions before God (I keep up an ongoing dialogue with Christ and His saints all day long), there is a danger of becoming stalemated by our own well-intentioned but nevertheless spiritually limiting requests. "No other desire is mine but to fulfill Thy will" is a statement I might never have thought to make, with a mind and heart so easily convoluted by earthly concerns.

Just this afternoon I was reading with my son, *Stories of Saints from the Prologue*, a spiral-bound book containing extracts from the lives of the saints compiled and adapted by Johanna Manley for seven-to-fourteen-year-olds. Today's passage was on the value of human suffering, something my son—and even his mother at times—still struggles to comprehend. Here is what the two of us discovered:

> *If the whole of your life has passed smoothly and without cares, weep for yourself. For the Gospel and the human experience assert with one voice that no one has, without great sufferings and trials, left behind any great work on earth or been glorified in heaven. If your earthly road has been bathed in sweat and tears for the obtaining of righteousness and truth, rejoice and be glad, for your reward will indeed be great in heaven. Never entertain the foolish thought that God has forsaken you. God knows exactly how much you can bear, and measures your sufferings and trials accordingly.* (Stories of Saints from the Prologue, *Bishop Nikolai Resource Center, Libertyville, IL, p. 79*)

Looking back on the past two decades, I am struck by how dramatically my life as a Christian was altered on my implantation into Orthodoxy. I mean, there are the obvious variants: priests, icons, confession, incense, all of which made my worship experience sound, smell, and feel very different from before. But beyond the outward manifestations, becoming Orthodox was like finally feeling satisfied after many years of attempting to ignore a subtle yet consistent hunger for something I couldn't quite put my finger on. It wasn't until I started regularly partaking of the same solid and satisfying nourishment originally offered to the followers of Jesus Christ almost two thousand years ago—including communion with

His saints; deliverance from my own biased and self-protective opinions; being grafted into a body of believers bound firmly together by history, persecution, monasticism, and the Holy Spirit—that I realized how truly ravenous I had been.

As with any religion or denomination, it is tempting at times to simply go through the motions; it is far too easy to forget just how magnanimous are the gifts we are receiving from God. Taken lightly, confession, Eucharist, prayer do me little good, not because God removes His presence from me, but rather because I am blinded from perceiving His Truth by my own choice to remain sidetracked and inattentive.

It is my responsibility, understanding all too well how dangerous and debilitating such self-imposed ignorance can be, to exemplify for my children the eternal benefits of being not only hearers but also doers of the Word. I can recall little (and that's being generous) about the geology class I took in high school, because the subject matter had no actual bearing on my everyday experiences; all of the studied facts and terminology pooled shallowly on the surface of my brain (just until the exam was over) without ever successfully permeating my long-term memory.

It is my deep desire that this not happen to my children with regard to the Orthodox Church. How do I present to them both the mysterious and practical aspects of our Orthodox theology in a way that would filter effectively through the denseness of rampant materialism and a universal preoccupation with the physical here and now? What are some ways I can help each of my children take ownership of their faith, to make that shift from a familial belief to a personal one?

I believe the answers to those questions are found primarily in their dad's and my relationship with them, with each other, and with the friends, acquaintances, and strangers we come into contact with. The more often we ourselves are seen drawing from the depths of a Christianity unstripped of its rich and fertile Tradition in order to overcome our temptations to be selfish, dishonest, or unjust, the more indispensable Orthodoxy will seem to our children.

Fr. Peter Gillquist wrote an excellent article for AGAIN Magazine in the summer of 2004 entitled, "Raising Children Who Believe: Five Steps We Took as Christian Parents," which points directly to the importance of mothers and fathers investing time and effort in building up strong relationships with their kids. In the beginning of this piece, Fr. Peter reveals his own motivation for making the spiritual lives of his six children a top priority:

My wife Marilyn and I both committed our lives to Christ while we were students at the University of Minnesota. One evening Dr. Bob Smith, a professor at Bethel College in St. Paul, talked on marriage and the family. Somewhere during his talk he created a picture that was indelibly etched in my mind. He said, "One day I'm going to stand before the judgment seat of Christ as a father, and my goal is to have my wife and children by my side, saying, 'Lord, we're all present and accounted for. Here's Mary, here's Steve, here's Johnny, we're all here.'" That night, I prayed, "Lord, that's what I want when I get married and have children—that we might all enter Your eternal Kingdom intact."

The rest of the article goes on to list and explain five of the ways he and Marilyn were able to raise six children who as adults have stayed active in the Orthodox Church:

1. *Make your family a priority.*
2. *Tell your children of God's faithfulness.*

3. *Love your spouse.*
4. *Never discipline out of anger.*
5. *Help your children discern God's will.*

What strikes me about these suggestions is how emotionally connected one would have to stay with one's family members in order to even begin laying a permanent foundation of faith within one's household. By putting our children's needs ahead of our own, talking constantly and conversationally about Christ, speaking respectfully and adoringly to our husbands, calmly yet consistently correcting misbehavior, and praying with our children for wisdom and clarity regarding their future, we make manifest for them the true nature of Christ, who is patient, generous, and forgiving.

Asceticism void of tenderness and unconditional love can paint an image in our children's minds of a God who is harsh and unapproachable. "If you are a zealot," writes Fr. Peter, "you may be tempted to force-feed them until they become rebels. I met a few men in seminary who were there not because they wanted to be, or even because God had called them; rather, they came to please their parents. And that's scary."

It takes a lot of concentration, I have discovered, and consistent forethought to find as many opportunities as possible in the ordinary exchanges with our children to validate our dedication both to them and to Christ. On a daily basis, for example, I must restrain myself and the unconstructive criticism poised to leap off my tongue due to tiredness and frustration by using the Jesus Prayer, out loud, in front of my kids. Before reacting, ideally, I step away from the mess or the look of defiance, make the sign of the cross, and state plainly, "Lord, have mercy on me, a sinner!" I ask for help right then and there to make a better decision than the one I know I am about to make.

The family member I am dealing with watches with a great deal of respect for the process that is hopefully keeping mom from losing her temper. It is a solid confirmation, to all of us, that God's grace and wisdom will be generously bestowed on those who ask for it with purity of heart. It is but one way to make the abstract conceivable and relevant to every area of our lives.

The Orthodox Faith can and should be more than just reverently admired for its vast symbolism and splendor on a Sunday morning. I can have no greater ambition than to make obvious to Elijah, Priscilla, Benjamin, and Mary the necessity of clinging desperately yet also joyfully to the Church and all of her ascetical resources, in order to find purpose and definitive fulfillment in each trivial and weighty incident they will encounter while here on earth. Even better than a Christian education is an enduring devotion to the Father and the Son and the Holy Spirit, now and ever and unto ages of ages. Even better than words are living illustrations of Trinity-inspired love and self-control.

Chapter Twelve

Inspiration

*L*ast May, I received a phone call from my nine-year-old son, Elijah, but I couldn't understand what he was saying due to his intermittent sobbing. "I'm in trouble," he was whispering (I think), "but I'm not sure why."

Elijah's teacher got on the phone. "Mrs. Sabourin, we've had an incident."

My chest tightened; my heart rate quickened. "What's going on?"

After Columbine and Virginia Tech, in the aftermath of too many horrific occurrences involving senseless brutality and young people in our public schools, strict rules were set in place and uniformly enforced. "I really don't think your son meant any harm," purred Mrs. H., "but unfortunately, we didn't have a choice. It is school policy that if any student makes a threat of any kind, that threat will be taken seriously and the student evaluated by a counselor."

"It's just protocol," was the underlying message I was receiving, as in, "Your fears about the darkening of your son's reputation sound awfully paranoid for the situation at hand." I was assured that the episode had been investigated and deemed innocuous. But Elijah, still raw with inexperience, was only beginning to come to terms with the shame and confusion accompanying those accusations, accusations of a type of violence he'd never previously been exposed to in thought, word, or deed. "If only you knew him as I do," I briefly contemplated mentioning, but just as quickly decided against it, lest such a sentiment be interpreted as biased, overly meddlesome, or spitefully ignorant.

It was some time before Elijah felt comfortable telling me exactly what had happened. "At recess we'd play tag, boys against girls," he began. "This one kid, Stephanie [not her real name], is a really fast runner and we'd tease each other about whose team was better, hers or mine. I like Stephanie, she's funny—she's my friend. I should have been paying attention in music class but I got bored and so, to be silly, I doodled on a handout, 'Destroy Stephanie,' and showed it to the person next to me, who laughed and then passed it down the row. Stephanie giggled too, but then my teacher grabbed the paper, and then ran and got another teacher, and then they both took me out into the hallway and had me sit in a desk for like an hour waiting to talk to a lady about my 'threatening' behavior. I was so confused, Mom. I felt yucky and really embarrassed. I cried, but I don't think the other kids saw me."

"Is this Mrs. P.?" I'd asked on that day in May, all anxious and edgy. "I'm Molly Sabourin, Elijah's mom." And I was ready to defend with a vengeance my tender, squirmy, and verbally precocious child until the counselor cut me off with just a hint of irritation in her otherwise calming demeanor.

"Oh my goodness, Mrs. Sabourin, this whole situation is just nothing but ridiculous. I have three boys of my own and they are forever 'destroying' each other and their fictitious enemies. Yes, we have a zero-tolerance policy when it comes to threats against the school, but in this case it was obvious your son had no intention of hurting anyone. He was horrified, quite frankly, and I did my best to help him realize that the entire affair was just a huge misunderstanding. I'd advise you not to question Elijah unless he brings it up himself. I promised him that it was over and not worth fretting about."

But what if she hadn't—hadn't promised him or appeased me? What if someday Elijah, or his siblings, or even Troy and I are pegged as a threat to peace and democracy—not because of a foolish mistake, for crossing a line inadvertently, but rather for purposefully adhering to our Orthodox Christian beliefs at the expense of evolving American values that keep time with dangerous whims born of self-enlightenment? I worry for my kids; this world is changing rapidly, growing increasingly hostile towards truth. There will come a day when opportunities are lost, freedoms restricted, reputations tainted by a refusal to compromise or espouse what was once viewed as sin but has now been gussied up and repackaged as open-mindedness. It is highly possible that when such a day arrives, justice will elude our "bigoted" family. So, what then?

Elijah's incident and the feelings it aroused in me came back to me as we prepared for the Feast of the Dormition, when the Orthodox Church commemorates the Lord taking up His Mother Mary into heaven after her death, which brought her rest from a fruitful yet often excruciating life. "In giving birth, you preserved your virginity; in falling asleep you did not forsake the world, O Theotokos," we sang as a family. I chanted the Troparion slowly, so my children could clearly make out the words, which, as usual, I believed in but had a difficult time making penetrate my present circumstances.

Mary, Theotokos: There is so much I simply cannot comprehend about her multifaceted identity as the Mother of God. The moment she willingly accepted that role would mark the demise of her public persona. From that day forth, her morality, convictions, and pious character would be called into question. She would have been isolated enough, both raising and being raised by God, without the added stigma of having her selflessness mocked by nearly impossible-to-defy innuendos that suggested Mary was but a slave to her own base desires. "Let it be to me," she said, "according to your word," and the bar was set for all of us who'd dare to swallow the Fire, the passions-searing inferno that is Christ.

But for Mary, that was only the beginning. Thirty-three years later came the real trial. Imagine being a witness to the torturing and murder of the one who was not only your Son but your supposed Savior. The despair would be immeasurable, unfathomable, unbearable. After all she'd already surrendered to play a part in the restoration of man's communion with the living God, her burning hope, which had kept her focused on the bigger picture, was inexplicably snuffed out with Jesus' final declaration of "It is finished."

"So, what now?" she must have wondered in misery.

Not too long ago, I felt justified keeping the Virgin Mary in her place as but a shell whose flesh was preordained to house temporarily the incarnate God-man, who alone was worthy of all my praise and reverence. As far as I knew, there were only two options: either ignore Mary or commit heresy by exalting her to the same level as Jesus, thereby detracting from His salvific work on the Cross.

Knowing what I know as an Orthodox believer, however, what I've been privileged to discover through Orthodox teaching concerning a third choice—one so biblically sound and logical and compelling that every other alternative now seems to me to be lacking in fullness and substance when viewed in light of it—it makes perfect theological sense that the continual remembrance of Mary's faithfulness to her Lord, throughout trials more straining and demanding than any other human being has ever encountered, is absolutely necessary for a complete experience of the Faith as it was originally lived out by the apostles. Archbishop Dmitri of Dallas and the South wrote the following concerning our veneration of Mary:

> *The Orthodox Church honors and venerates the Virgin Mary as "more honorable than the Cherubim and more glorious without compare than the Seraphim . . ." Her name is mentioned in every service, and her intercession before the throne of God is asked. She is given the title of "Theotokos" (Greek for "Birth-giver-of-God"), as well as "Mother of God". She has a definite role in Orthodox Christianity, and can in no way be considered an instrument which, once used, was laid aside and forgotten. . . . The Virgin Mary in the Orthodox view is not regarded as a mediatrix or co-redemptress. She is an intercessor for us, and the content of prayer addressed to her is a request for her intercession. The Orthodox concept of the Church is the basic reason for the invocation of the Theotokos and all the saints. The Militant Church on earth and the Victorious Church in heaven are intimately bound together in love. If it is proper for one sinner to ask another sinner to pray for him, how much more fitting it must be to ask the saints already glorified and near the throne of God to pray for us. Surely, they know something of what goes on here, for else how could there be rejoicing in heaven over the conversion of one sinner? (Luke 15:10) The saints in heaven are equals of the angels (Luke 20:36), who are used by God in the accomplishment of His*

purpose (Acts 12:7). (http://www.orthodoxresearchinstitute.
org/articles/dogmatics/dmitri_veneration_mary.htm)

We have lovely hymns in the Orthodox Church; my favorite is sung to Mary during the Paschal Divine Liturgy. For three days she mourned; for the whole of her life she remained obedient in the midst of ridicule, prejudice, and persecution. I get chills when the time comes to travel with the angels to our grieving Theotokos, to share with her the glorious news of our triumph over death through Her Son's Resurrection:

> *The Angel cried to the Lady full of grace,*
> *Rejoice, O pure Virgin!*
> *Again, I say rejoice!*
> *Your Son is risen from His three days in the tomb!*
> *With Himself He has raised all the dead.*
> *Rejoice, O ye people!*
> *Shine, O new Jerusalem!*
> *The glory of the Lord has shone on you.*
> *Exult now, exult and be glad, O Zion!*
> *Be radiant, O pure Theotokos,*
> *In the Resurrection of your Son!*

I am forever on a quest to replace fear with courage, doubt with assuredness, my own agendas—for both myself and my children—with the same pliability and submissiveness the Virgin Mary displayed when stepping up to embrace a role that would open for every one of us the door to redemption, eternal life, and freedom from the hell of our own transgressions. As a woman, I am thankful for my newly acquired intimacy with femininity in its purest form, with an example of sacred nobility that in every possible way outshines the dullness inherent in vanity, insecurity, and self-gratification—with the righteous, victorious, and most honorable Mother of Christ Jesus.

We have within our Orthodox Tradition many brave women, strong women, genuinely beautiful women to look up to. We have valuable opportunities at our disposal not only to learn about their steadfastness and unique contributions throughout history, but also, through Christ, to commune with them—here, in the present. For years, I gave lip service to the extraordinariness of heaven intersecting with earth in this manner. It's taken awhile, however, for me to truly long for a connection with the "great cloud of witnesses" Paul refers to in Hebrews, surrounding us and encouraging us to press onward.

The other day I received an invitation from a cyber friend to join an online photo-sharing group called "People with Icons," which was inspired by a lovely set of photographs entitled, "Women with Icons," created by the photographer Jocelyn Mathewes. The idea was that we would each take a picture of ourselves with an icon of our patron saint and upload it for others to look at.

After viewing some touching contributions from my fellow group members, I was inspired to submit something of my own, and so I climbed the stairs to our prayer corner to find our image of the Holy Prophetess Anna. But upon approaching the far wall, adorned liberally with heavenly reminders of what truly represents the "one thing needful," I looked St. Anna square in the eyes and then, not without shame, retreated. I wasn't yet ready, I discovered, for such a project.

When we were joining the Orthodox Church, my husband

and I were told to choose a saint, a patron saint whose name we would take as our own, whose identity we would try our best to emulate. We felt drawn to St. Simeon and the Prophetess Anna; I liked that they'd met the Christ child simultaneously, and it was special to me to have an icon featuring both of them together. These patron saints would pray for us, a concept that was new to me yet intriguing.

I was at a loss, however, as to how to form a more intimate relationship with my saint in particular. Throughout the decade that followed, I would hear her name when I opened my mouth to receive the Eucharist. I ended my prayers with "through the intercessions of the Prophetess Anna" and all the other patron saints connected with our various family members. I revered her; I believed wholeheartedly in her dedication to all of us on earth trying to work out our salvation with fear and trembling. But at that moment, standing face-to-face with her alone in our second-story hallway, the idea of posing with her for a photograph such as I would take with my best of friends, my mother or my aunt, seemed inappropriate.

I was long overdue in putting forth a concerted effort to better understand this most pious individual and through that acquired awareness, become more Christlike. Thus began my mission to uncover information and then meditate on its relevance to my life. I began to seek a way that I might soften the formality a bit and close the gap between us, which I had created through a lack of communication. Who was Anna, exactly, and which of her specific traits could I imitate and draw strength from? It would be well worth my time to find out.

The most obvious place to start was the Scriptures. In the Gospel of St. Luke I found the following summary of Anna's life:

Now there was one, Anna, a prophetess, the daughter of Phanuel, of the tribe of Asher. She was of a great age, and had lived with a husband seven years from her virginity; and this woman was a widow of about eighty-four years, who did not depart from the temple, but served God with fastings and prayers night and day. And coming in that instant she gave thanks to the Lord, and spoke of Him to all those who looked for redemption in Jerusalem. (Luke 2:36–38)

When I explain to you what struck me immediately upon combing that passage like a detective searching for clues, you will accurately assess that I am, unfortunately, somewhat pessimistic and in need of a faith-infused backbone. At a relatively young age, St. Anna lost her first and only husband to death. This is beyond significant to me, because I waste a lot of energy being afraid of that very scenario, at times to the point of emotional paralysis.

"What would I do? How would I go on?" I wonder, blinking back tears during a bout of insomnia while watching the chest of my own beloved spouse rise and fall steadily in sleep. Anna was once a wife, as I am a wife. It is probable she loved with the same intensity that I do the partner whose identity had fused together with her own and whose unexpected departure ripped a throbbing, open wound within her heart. Anna grieved, I am sure; she was most likely nervous about the future; but notice that the sorrow was not, by any means, the end of her story.

O Holy Prophetess Anna, you endured my greatest of fears, yet through the grace of God were not crushed and beaten down ever after. Please pray to Christ that I might take courage in your resilience and trust with all my soul in the wisdom of His plans.

It is hard for me to imagine, with all the breeziness and comfort I've grown accustomed to, being married to the Church, spending every waking moment suppressing the urge to forget that I am called upon to be perfect, just as God Himself is. Anna prayed, we are told, and fasted with fervor unknown to me. Her unrestrained commitment is like a mirror revealing the chasm between what I currently am and what I could be. But rather than taunting us with our weaknesses, the Prophetess Anna provides a respite from mediocrity, beaming like a lighthouse that leads away from the dangers of blindness and into safety.

St. Anna, I am tired, so very drained from fighting impulses to lie down and rest, to wallow in self-pity. Teach me, by your example, how to weather the tumult of my passions until at last I find the peace achieved through sacrifice.

My neighbor is depressed about finances, her moody children, and her strained marriage. And what do I have to offer her? A lot more than I actually give, which is usually a nodding head and a sympathetic expression. It's always sitting there on the tip of my tongue, the conversation about love—Christ's love specifically and how it transforms even the grimmest of situations. But what would she think of me if I unleashed that un-neutral bombshell? I suppose it shouldn't concern me, and in all actuality it should probably spill from my lips because my spirit cannot contain it—my gratitude and joy at having found the sacred pearl of great price (Matthew 13:45, 46).

How can unashamed convictions and impartiality walk hand-in-hand? Why am I so timid about openly speaking the truth? The Prophetess Anna, my holy namesake, was defined by her enthusiasm, her message about God and the necessity of repentance, which never wavered, never fluctuated, never watered itself down to appease the masses.

I need words and motivation; I want to want to share with others what I've experienced through the Church in terms of clarity, mercy, and a sense of purpose. You, O Prophetess Anna, were a mouthpiece until your last days on earth for what was and still is the very crux of all creation . . . for God. May your zeal get under my skin like a splinter that persistently irritates the normal goings-on of my daily routine. May I never settle for "good enough" when before me shines your tirelessly impeccable standard, so bright that anything less than a total commitment to the Faith I am trusting to save me feels only dull, cloudy, and unsatisfying.

How fortuitous, don't you think—that I was linked for all eternity to one whose spiritual muscles bulge where mine hang soft and limp, in need of some serious weight bearing? Or is nothing coincidental when it comes to salvation? Here's the honest truth—I need all the help I can get, and praise be to God for the tools He's set before us—including Eucharist, confession, and the earnest intercessions of His saints. Can I afford to take for granted any one of these pulsating lifelines through which nourishment is provided, as through the cord that attaches a baby to the sustenance of his mother? Well, there's a no-brainer . . . I think not. So how do I proceed in my quest for friendship and closeness with someone who's journeyed onward out of this life and into another beyond it? I suppose with her troparion—the hymn sung in St. Anna's honor on her day of commemoration, February 3:

*In the Temple you embraced as an infant God the Word who
   became flesh,
O glorious Elder Simeon, who held God in your arms;*

And also as a Prophetess the august Anna ascribed praise to Him.
We acclaim you as divine servants of Christ.

I should know this, I should recite it on a regular basis; I should anticipate our nameday instead of scratching my head two days after its passing, asking, "Hmm, now when was that again?" I should maintain an ongoing conversation, sharing my thoughts and insecurities along the way. I should remember that she is watching and witnessing my progression from a spineless observer to what I pray will be a bold and obvious beacon for Christ's glory. I should remember her utter joy at having met her God incarnate and be stimulated to rejoice likewise.

Pray to God for me, O Holy Anna, well-pleasing to God: for I turn to you, who are the speedy helper and intercessor for my soul.

I'll have my mother come over to give me a hand, to hold the camera while I position myself in a way that will visually, artistically represent my forging a connection with a reality that binds heaven to earth, sinners to saintliness, me to an ancestor who has completed her race and now stands at the finish line compelling me to keep moving forward. I will feel within my grasp the painted wood, a very touchable representation of that which blows my mind if I think about it too logically, instead of mystically or innocently like a child. I will use this opportunity, this invitation as a springboard to dive ever more deeply into the mysteries of the Church, into her bosom of magnificence and righteousness. I'm a slow yet willing learner who admits to a habit of foot-dragging but is now quite anxious to get started.

Holy Prophetess Anna, I implore you to bring my burdens, all my baggage and my blunders before that same Son of God you held with such reverence in your aged arms. Please beseech of Him that my vision be enhanced, that the scales on my eyes be lifted, that I might see you, know you, venerate you, and be wiser, braver, more confident because of it.

Forgive me for not asking this of you sooner.

Chapter Thirteen

Intercession

I was already pretty sure I couldn't hack it, even before the impending disaster that would only further verify my incompetence. Nine months earlier, having a second child had seemed like a wonderful idea, but that was before, when filtered and distant notions were too far off to affect reality.

As my due date loomed closer, difficult questions began sprouting like aggressive weeds, strangling buds in my garden of idealism. Two arms, I had counted while taking inventory of my mothering assets, two legs and one body—there wasn't enough of me, I suddenly realized, to go around. Elijah was a handful at two-and-a-half years old, the kind of toddler who was unimpressed by a furrowed brow or high-pitched warnings. He'd grown accustomed to the life we'd built together, one in which he was the center of my universe. I had just enough patience and stamina to keep one kid away from busy streets; how on earth would I ever leave the house, make a meal, or finish a thought with yet another dependent little one strapped permanently to my person by way of breastfeeding, a sling, or a rocking chair?

Fortunately, on Priscilla's arrival, I remembered that adoration, in most cases, overrides our fear of failure. "So this is why we keep reproducing," I thought to my infatuated self as I stroked the silky curls on my daughter's head. Thankfully, there was plenty of help available for those first two weeks; I was free to sit and bond with the baby.

Eventually, however, husbands return to their jobs and meals stop being delivered to your front door. Sooner than I would have liked, of course, I was alone again with my required domestic tasks and apprehensions. The days stuck at home stretched on interminably, as I was nervous to venture out of doors with just the three of us. When, a month into my new position as a mother of not one, but two children, I was invited to go shopping with my parents, I leapt at the opportunity and waited anxiously for the clock hands to turn in my favor.

It took a ridiculous amount of time to pack a diaper bag with all the burp cloths, extra clothing, pacifiers, and changing pads, but Priscilla and I were ready when our coach finally arrived in the form of a dark blue Passat. "Goodbye," I waved to Troy and Elijah, way overexcited about commonplace occurrences such as wearing jeans, seeing people I wasn't related to, and escaping the perimeters of our urban neighborhood. It was exactly what I needed: a moderately grand adventure.

Our destination that fateful evening was Ikea, a massive and magnificent Swedish-born shopping arena packed with wall hooks, storage bins, and lingonberries. For weeks I had been drooling over their catalogue, daydreaming about how much better life would be if only my kitchen and bedroom had more jars, tubs, and shelves to keep all of our accumulating junk in order. Having been sequestered for a while within our modest Chicago two-flat, I found the stimulation of actually ogling and touching in person that innovative (and much-coveted) merchandise somewhat intoxicating.

To my great relief, Priscilla was being an angel; she had slept soundly and silently in her car seat since entering the store. Perhaps this is why at first I didn't notice her absence. For the previous half hour, my mom and I had taken turns pushing my newborn in the cart, so when I turned to ask her opinion about a picture frame I was interested in purchasing and noticed that she was alone without my baby, I felt the hairs on the back of my neck stand on end.

"Wait, where is Priscilla?" I asked, to which she replied, "Honey, I thought you had her!" And the horror that ensued was indescribable.

I didn't think or calmly retrace my steps, I just ran. I ran and scanned the aisles, growing more and more distraught with each minute that passed by without finding her. I was nauseated and inconsolable, irrational and ashamed. "My daughter!" I was yelling with tears streaming down my face. "Please help me! I cannot find my daughter!"

An employee listened intently as my father described the situation. Immediately there was an announcement over the intercom: "Code Fifty-eight!" said a disembodied voice. "We are looking for a four-week-old infant last seen fifteen minutes ago on the third floor." All the doors were locked; gaping patrons pointed and whispered, "There she is, the girl who lost her baby."

Either moments or hours later (I can't recall), I came across a crowd protectively guarding my abandoned child. In the exact place I'd started from was a still-sleeping Priscilla, oblivious to the drama she'd been the center of. Had I turned back a few feet after talking to my mom, instead of taking off hysterically in the opposite direction, I would have seen her, I would have avoided that entire humiliating nightmare. But

I didn't pause, I panicked, and under the scrutiny of fellow Ikea customers I left trembling that night, ready to throw in the towel and let someone else more responsible rear the children I obviously had no business raising myself. It was the first of many times I would seriously doubt my aptitude as a parent.

Evidently I eventually recovered, going on to produce an additional son and daughter. Time and duty numbed the sting of those frightful memories, and I stepped up to the plate to take another crack at molding thoughtful, resourceful, and productive members of society out of the malleable and reliant souls within my care. I've pranced through months laced with pride and satisfaction as my growing children displayed intelligence, compassion, and creativity without my prompting. "It's working," I have concluded, "I do have brilliant, obedient, God-fearing kids. I guess I am a decent mother after all."

And I offer up to Christ the appropriate prayers of praise and thanksgiving for all the blessings a family affords—until, that is, there's a shift in the serenity of our household. Behavior I find appalling from my five- or two-year-old, a nine-year-old son's inexplicable undercurrent of anger and disrespect, a daughter's loathing of all chores (and her siblings) can instantaneously renew the angst of being powerless to ensure a romantic outcome—can knock me forcibly over the head again with accusations from myself to myself regarding negligence, misaligned priorities, and a general lack of skill. "I stink at this," I moan while conjuring up numerous outlandish and unpleasant future scenarios involving four selfish, lazy, spiritually ambivalent adults each bearing my last name and fair complexion.

"You can't possibly know where to begin if you don't start your morning with a fervent entreaty to God for direction and wisdom," says my priest after every confession. I am, unfortunately, an agonizingly slow learner. It's just that sometimes that answer seems so pat and far less palpable than, say, a how-to book on managing your home and the people in it. I should know by this point that Christ abides in the subtleties, but I'm a sucker for what is loud and most blatant in the here and now—or more specifically, my needy family and our deficiencies. I've overpacked, is what I've done; I've crammed morbid fears, weighty expectations, and popular opinions into my already full heart, and now I'm wondering why my stride is so easily broken.

We parents are such obvious targets for discouragement and despair because it rarely crosses our minds that when loving, pleasing, and fretting over our family members takes precedence over the fostering of our faith, we are essentially rejecting Christ's invitation to take His yoke upon us and find rest. Why not just claim the irrefutable truth that I am so unbelievably imperfect and in constant need of divine supervision? Why not spare myself the exact same cyclical patterns? All this running around in circles feeling lost and scared and aggravated will only keep me from finding the confidence, the joy, the source of astuteness made amply available for those brave enough to slow down, release their baggage, and humbly receive it. Why not stop already with the negative assumptions and start anticipating the grace we've been promised?

On both my bad days and my good days, I am still a mother. Whether I'm sick or healthy, optimistic or depressed, fulfilled or empty, I am responsible for raising the children in my care. What this basically guarantees is that many of my parenting moments and decisions I will feel great about, and many others I will grieve over and regret for years to come. No matter what goals I accomplish outside of mothering, my overall worth and self-esteem will still, inevitably, be all wrapped up in the behaviors my kids adopt for themselves, and their long-term emotional and spiritual health (or lack thereof), if I'm not careful. It is so very, very difficult not to take personally the childish disobedience that, let's face it, is often quite humiliating. It will be even harder, I am assuming, as they get older and become more independent, to watch helplessly as they make choices I may find foolish or even dangerous, despite my sound advice to proceed otherwise.

And then there is mortality, with its quiet yet constant threat that maybe years from now, or maybe tomorrow, everything will unravel. Love laced with dread; love strangled by horrific possibilities; an unexplained ache while embracing my child or waving goodbye to my spouse; the fear, contaminating joy so sweet, whispering in my ear, "You would die, wither up and waste away if that baby, that preteen, that husband left this world before you"—these are not congruent with a victorious Resurrection. This fear of death, fear of failure, fear of despair, I want to examine, repent of, and obliterate as an heir of the living Christ.

Abraham walked with Isaac up a mountain. Abraham, fondling the dagger in his cloak, perhaps slicing his finger over the blade, marched onward toward the unthinkable, guided only by a pious devotion to God. I can tolerate this story when that same God is foremost on my mind and in my heart. But when the order is reversed, when my children tower over my Creator in my affections, that story both offends and disturbs me.

"Why must you love God more?" ask my jealous children in unison while dissecting the priorities I try my best to keep from getting jumbled. "We love you more than anything!"

"Don't you see?" I answer, as much to myself as to them. "My own love is broken and imperfect. Only by loving God first can I love you best—can I open my hands, keep a healthy perspective, and give you freedom."

Possession is tricky because it feels like devotion, even as it smothers and frets. Possession keeps one busy with paying bills, charting goals, changing sheets on a bunk bed. It tells you that if you try hard enough, worry obsessively enough, and make just the right plans and resolutions, it will all work out in the end; it will all come together just as you devised.

There is no room in this soul for Christ and anything else. To add my own agenda is to compromise the purity of my faith. To desire nothing but sunny days and a woundless existence is to close my mind to the will of God. There is so much evil in this world. Just trying to keep on top of it while wagging my head in disbelief can be a full-time occupation. The longer I look, the more effort I invest into stockpiling my basement with generators, water bottles, and bird-flu vaccines, the less confident my prayers become. It is hard to pray and duct-tape windows simultaneously; it is hard to long for heaven when your one ambition in life is to keep your family anchored to this earth.

If I could bottle the courage that springs up in me during the Paschal Liturgy when I sing along with Jesus to Mary, the Theotokos: "Do not lament me, O Mother, seeing me in the tomb, for I shall arise and be eternally glorified as God," I would drink of it continually. I would bathe in it, cleansing my tormented thoughts with the healing promise of the crucified Christ. I would shout at the top of my lungs, echoing with transcendental volume off the walls of an empty tomb, the words of St. John Chrysostom:

O death, where is thy sting? O Hades, where is thy victory?
Christ is risen, and you, O death, are annihilated! Christ is

risen, and the evil ones are cast down! Christ is risen, and the
angels rejoice! Christ is risen, and life is liberated!

If I do not believe that it is achievable to find complete liberation from my bondage to anxiety, self-doubt, vanity, and pride—all the mothering vices that distract me from a God-given potential for peace—there is no point, really, in continuing with the ascetical efforts the Orthodox Church prescribes. Fasting, confessing, and participating in divine services are not merely sacred ways to pass the time; they are meant, rather, to totally transform and renew us from within.

It's a completely unfeasible balancing act, trying to nurture our children emotionally, provide for them physically, discipline them consistently, and keep them away from dangers we can't possibly know how to prepare for ahead of time. I know I've lost my bearings when I am running around in circles, fretting obsessively over minutiae, dropping balls, and losing sleep to late-night worries. That miserable feeling of hopelessness is like a warning signal screaming, "Danger, danger, danger, you have lost your Christ-centered frame of reference!" If my entire sense of well-being revolves solely around the children and their opinions of me—around their moods, their health, or the organizational state of their bedrooms—I will never garner the stamina necessary to make wise decisions rather than easy or popular ones.

"From this day, from this hour, from this minute," said St. Herman of Alaska, "let us love God above all else." It is so difficult as a mother to accept that "all else" includes our families.

"And it certainly doesn't get easier," say my own parents, "because adult children get married and then you have their spouses and your grandchildren to fret over. It was simpler when your problems could be fixed by establishing rules or by us physically, emotionally, or even financially intervening, but now when you struggle, our hearts just break for you and we sometimes feel so helpless."

I can remember in college calling home when things got tough. "I'll never get through this semester," I would wail. "I'm lonely. I'm scared. I'm totally broke!" My poor mom and dad would then carry around on their shoulders the added weight of my dramas, never realizing that I was merely venting and that two hours later I would be sailing through an assignment or grabbing some sugared-up coffee with friends. They wouldn't know I had recovered, because of course I'd forgotten to tell them.

Nowadays, they assure me, they are making a conscious effort to, in the healthiest way possible, create a buffer between themselves and my brother and me. They are putting all the energy they would previously have expended on worrying about things they have absolutely no control over, into turning us over to God by way of prayer and meditation on Christ. Romans 8:28 declares that "all things work together for good to those who love God, to those who are the called according to His purpose." We can only digest such a statement if we are actively pursuing truth. Otherwise, the rejections, illnesses, or injustices our children endure will seem intolerable, pointless, and wicked.

St. Simeon the New Theologian wrote in his "Practical and Theological Precepts":

> *A man who, instead of avoiding and running away from sufferings of the heart produced by fear of eternal torment, willingly accepts them in his heart . . . will be determined, as he progresses, to tighten this bond ever more and more, and will thus advance more quickly. It will lead him to the presence of*

the King of kings. When this comes to pass, then, as soon as he sees, however dimly, the glory of God, his bonds—fear—will at once fall off, his executioner will hasten away and his heart's grief will turn into joy which will become in him a fountain of life or a spring for ever gushing forth: physically—rivers of tears; spiritually—peace, meekness and unspeakable delight, together with courage and free and unhindered readiness to strive towards every fulfillment of God's commandments. (Writings from the Philokalia on Prayer of the Heart, Faber & Faber, pp. 112–113)

Do I not want this for myself and for my family—to be freed from the bonds of fear in order to "strive towards every fulfillment of God's commandments" with meekness, peace, and delight? Yes, my gosh, of course yes. But such a desire must be vigorously tended or it will wilt under the strain of competing base cravings for my children's continuous comfort and worldly success. I will, most likely, have to fight my entire life to filter out spiritually unproductive stimuli and unearth within my soul, created for communion with Christ Jesus, a confidence that transcends my faults, fears, and failures.

Just recently I penned the following letter to my children, in which I honestly examined my last nine years as a mom. I wanted to draw a line in the sand, so to speak, by openly acknowledging the pitfalls I am most susceptible to in order to name, claim, and release them and move beyond an enlightening past into a purposeful future.

> *Dearest loved ones,*
>
> *I am writing to let you know that I am sorry. I am sorry that I've spent so much, too much time agonizing over my own deficiencies when all you've ever wanted was my attention and for me to be at peace. It started when you were babies and I*

came home, stayed home all day. My own mother, and her mother before her, had been so very efficient at washing clothes and mending them, making savory and comforting meals out of leftovers and pantry staples, mopping floors, weeding a garden—keeping house. So I waited, waited for the instincts to kick in that would help to control the chaos which had swallowed our small apartment; I waited and waited and waited, but they totally stood me up—they totally stood me up, and so I read.

You have no idea, my darlings, how much pressure there is on a young mother to keep everything in order: your behavior, the grocery list, our messes. I borrowed and purchased used manuals on bread baking, clutter clearing, schedule keeping, and discipline. I devoted myself to the process of transformation—to becoming my friend who served homemade granola and flax meal muffins to her toddler, my neighbor with the labeled bins and laminated chore charts, the woman in my church with the hand-sewn Nativity calendar, to becoming everyone and yet no one in particular.

I apologize for the ruined laundry, the hundreds of resolutions I could never follow through on, for teaching you nary a handicraft or foreign language; I apologize for shutting the garage door on our minivan. Somewhere along the way it ceased to be about your welfare and became more about my own pride, insecurities, and envy. I wasted hours on treating the symptoms instead of the cause of my discontent. I'm a wreck, children, when I cease to nail my flesh to the fear of Christ—which is different, mind you, from talking about Him or making references to His goodness in conversation. When I reach the point where nothing truly matters but the obtaining of my salvation—when my only motivation for speaking, redirecting, beautifying, entertaining, forgiving, writing, sacrificing, spending, befriending, volunteering, educating, and worshiping is love for Christ, plain and simple—I will lose myself and then rid myself of the pesky expectations so irrelevant to the existence I was created for.

So here's the deal, my sons and daughters: Your mother is not gifted in the art of domesticity; she is impulsive and somewhat flighty, quite capable of getting lost in her own neighborhood. Though I may serve the same five basic dinners to you over and over again, though your Batman suitcase may always be stuffed with mismatched socks whose partners I've misplaced and will most likely never find, though I no longer have any idea what is molding inside the Tupperware containers in the refrigerator, there is still plenty I can offer you as a parent:

I promise that I will stay loyal, devoted, and invested in your lives. I promise to own up to my own mistakes. I will talk with you about anything; don't be ashamed or embarrassed to approach me. I will enjoy you. I will try to be more patient. I will focus my energies on becoming less obsessed with the ever-rotating, new and grandiose schemes that promise to improve my experience as a homemaker, and more consistent with our family prayers and my personal prayers and remembering those who are struggling with pain or loneliness. I will do my best to keep all our daily frustrations in perspective.

I used to think that I just wasn't mom material, which was true, I found out, if by "mom material" I meant "Stepford wife." But raising mute and passive offspring without the messiness of free will to make things complicated now sounds awfully morose to me. I am certainly no expert on childrearing, but I do believe (finally!) that I am the best mother for you, Elijah, Priscilla, Benjamin, and Mary. I believe that I will one day be held accountable not for how successful I was at getting the poster paint out of your jean shorts, but for how much effort I put forth toward your spiritual development. I believe you have revealed to me just as much, if not more, than I've passed

on to you so far about faith and resilience and mercy—about
the second, fifth, millionth chance we are given to get it right.
Thank you for that and for everything.
   I am here for you . . . always.

Love,
Mom

About the Author

Molly Sabourin is a writer living in Indiana with her husband, Troy, and their four children. She has a B.A. in education from Moody Bible Insitute. Her work has appeared in such publications as *AGAIN*, *Salvo*, and *MomSense*. Molly is also a columnist for *The Handmaiden*, a quarterly journal for Orthodox Christian women, and a regular podcaster for Ancient Faith Radio.

Listen to Molly Sabourin's podcast,
"Close to Home," on

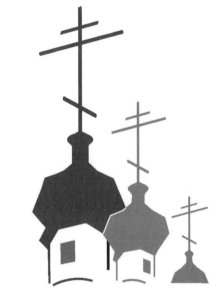

ANCIENT FAITH RADIO
www.ancientfaithradio.com

Recommended Reading

Lynette's Hope: The Witness of Lynette Katherine Hoppe's Life and Death *edited by Fr. Luke Veronis*

Lynette Hoppe's life and death touched hundreds, if not thousands, of lives as she served as a missionary in Albania, succumbing to cancer in 2006. Close family friend and fellow OCMC missionary Fr. Luke Veronis retells the story of her life, then lets her writing speak for itself. In frank and poignant prose, Lynette's diaries, newsletters, and website chronicled her struggles in the "valley of the shadow" as she faced impending death. Her radical faith and love for Christ transformed the tragedy of a young mother's untimely death into a powerful witness to the love and saving power of her Lord. Those who witnessed Lynette's passing agree that hers was truly a "beautiful death," and readers of her story can only agree. ◆ Trade paper, 272 pages plus 16-page photo section (ISBN: 978-1-888212-99-0) CP Order No. 007515— $17.95

Royal Monastic: Princess Ileana of Romania *by Bev. Cooke*

The life of a princess isn't all fun-filled travel, magnificent banquets, handsome princes, and beautiful clothes. It's also devotion to duty, sacrifice for your people, and a lot of just plain hard work. And if your country happens to suffer two world wars and a communist takeover in your lifetime, it means danger and suffering, exile and heartache as well.

Princess Ileana of Romania endured all this and more. But her deeply rooted Orthodox faith saw her through it all, and eventually led her in her later years to the peaceful repose of monasticism. But that life included sacrifice and hard work as well, because as Mother Alexandra she was called to build the first English-language Orthodox women's monastery in the United States—the Monastery of the Transfiguration in Ellwood City, Pennsylvania.

Princess Ileana's story is a thrilling tale of love and loss, danger and rescue, sacrifice and reward. Her inspiring life stands as a beacon of faith and holiness for young women of all times and nations to follow. ◆ Trade paper, 200 pages (ISBN: 978-1-888212-32-7) CP Order No. 007606— $15.95

Pictures of God: A Child's Guide to Understanding Icons
by John Kosmas Skinas
When the Son of God came down from heaven to become a man like us, He made it possible for us to see Him, touch Him, and make pictures of Him—pictures which we call icons. This little book brings God and His saints vividly into children's lives through icons, explaining in the simplest terms what each icon means and what the role of these holy pictures—and the holy stories and people they depict—can be in our lives.

The colorful pages of *Pictures of God* are perfect for occupying little hands in church, for explaining the world of icons in the first years of Sunday school, and for read-aloud time with little ones at home. ◆ Paperback, 32 pages (ISBN: 978-1-888212-58-7) CP Order No. 007614— $10.95

Seasons of Grace: Reflections on the Church Year
by Donna Farley
There is enormous tension between entering fully into the church year and the pressures of society. We sometimes find ourselves walking a tightrope between what we think is the ideal of a holy life and the demands of our postmodern world. The beauty of the church seasons is that they teach us how to balance our life. The Christian life is a whole life, an expansive life, a life in Christ, who gives Himself for the life of the world. This collection is author Donna Farley's own view from the tightrope. These short yet thoughtful reflections, written in an insightful and sometimes humorous style, will help weave together the great feasts into the fabric of our lives. ◆ Trade paper, 195 pages (ISBN: 978-1-888212-50-1) CP Order No. 005658— $14.95

Gender: Men, Women, Sex, and Feminism
by Frederica Mathewes-Green
This anthology provides a selection of popular speaker and writer Frederica Mathewes-Green's best writings on contemporary issues relating to gender. Her original and thoughtful insights are expressed in a style that is fresh, personal, and frequently humorous. She examines modern-day challenges from a perspective of ancient wisdom, as one who seeks to be deeply grounded in the faith of the early Christian Church. ◆ Trade paper, 184 pages (ISBN: 978-1-888212-31-0) CP Order No. 005660— $15.95

All books listed are available from Conciliar Press at www.conciliarpress.com, or call 800-967-7377.